Reading
GOD'S MIND

Reading
GOD'S MIND

His Thoughts for Every Life Situation

D O T T I E
E I C H H O R N

WinePressPublishing
Great Books, Defined.

ISBN 13: 978-1-60615-034-4
ISBN 10: 1-60615-034-0
Library of Congress Catalog Card Number: 2009941915

Dedication

In memory of my mother.

Thank You

To Dick for your support.

God created *you*. *You* are His child;
He is *your* heavenly Father.
He loves *you* so much.
He gave *you* an instruction book to help *you* through
your earthly life; it is the Bible.
He wants the *best for you*!

CONTENTS

INTRODUCTION

The *best* book to read is the Bible! Many years ago I was told this, but, of course, I was too busy and liked the way things were going. I had a job. I had friends. I had my health. I read inspirational books. My life seemed good.

I belonged to a book club in which we read a variety of books. During that time those words came back to me: "The *best* book to read is the Bible!" So when I was in my forties, I finally decided to read the Bible.

I started at the beginning. Some chapters didn't pique my interest as others did, and I certainly didn't understand everything. But there were so many passages and stories that grabbed my heart that I started on a journey, a journey toward an intimate relationship with God.

This journey, which I am still on, has changed my life and has given me peace, joy, and blessings too numerous to count. My only regret is that I was so absorbed in myself that I did not read the Bible earlier in my life. I would have been able to handle my daily situations in a godly fashion that would have blessed me.

After my mother passed away, I started to read the Bible from the beginning again. As I was reading, different passages jumped off the pages, so I started writing them down. Before I knew it, I could see how the passages fit into different categories. Reading God's words filled me with so much hope that it became my passion for everyone to read the Bible, so that they too can experience the benefits of knowing God.

This book is for everyone, young, old, and in-between—for the person who has never heard of God or Jesus, for the person who has heard of God or Jesus but ignored Him, and for the person who has heard of God or Jesus and knows something about Him and wants to know more.

Have you ever thought about why you haven't read the Bible? If you have thought about it, which of these sound like your reasons?

- It isn't the thing to do.
- I will be too religious.
- Religion has a bad connotation.
- God or Jesus is not politically correct.
- I might be unpopular.
- I am afraid to change my lifestyle or am satisfied with the way things are.
- I don't understand it. There are too many antiquated words.
- I don't have time. (Is it that you don't have time or that you want to do something else?)

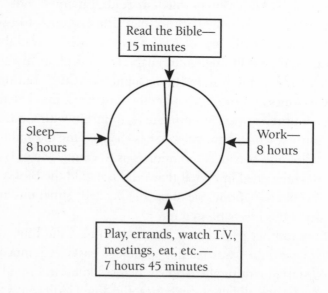

This diagram shows what a small part of your day fifteen minutes actually is!

If you knew that reading the Bible fifteen minutes a day

- would make your life better;
- would give you instructions and prepare you on how to handle disappointments, heartaches, persecution, illness, marriage, child's behavior, loss, and all that arises in your life;
- wouldn't make you change but would give you the option to change;
- would expand your knowledge and give you wisdom;
- can equip you to receive blessings;
- would explain the difference between death and eternal life;
- would encourage you to have a relationship with God;
- would give you great literature, which surpasses many scholarly writings;
- would give you many stories that happened to ordinary people before, during, and after Jesus Christ;
- would bring you joy;
- would reveal God's love and the importance of love;

would you read it then?

Let me introduce you to God through some passages from the Bible. Each of the chapters in this book has a main theme and provides verses from the Bible on that theme. You may start reading with any chapter, since none is dependent on the others. My prayer is that God's words will inspire you to read more of the Bible, so that you will have a personal relationship with Him.

Some tips as you read: Throughout the passages you will find capitalized nouns and pronouns referring to God, such as *Me*, *My*, *Mine*, *Him*, *Himself*, *His*, *You*, *Your*, *Maker*, and *Almighty*. Also, you will see the word *Selah* in a few of the passages. It is a Hebrew word that you may find at the end of a verse in the book of Psalms. According to the *The New American Heritage Dictionary*, this word has an unknown meaning and is "thought to be a term indicating a pause or rest."

As you read the passages from the Bible in this book, remember:

It is God's inspired Word.   "All Scripture is given by inspiration of God."
(2 Timothy 3:16 NKJV)

God never lies.   "For the word of the LORD is right, and all His work is done in truth."
(Psalm 33:4 NKJV)

"It is impossible for God to lie."
(Hebrews 6:18 NKJV)

"God, who cannot lie."
(Titus 1:2 NKJV)

God never changes.   "For I am the LORD, I do not change."
(Malachi 3:6 NKJV)

In Appendix 1, you will find "Study Guide Questions for Discussion," which are great for book clubs, Christian groups, families, or just a few friends. You may also discuss some of the questions after each chapter. Feel free to mark, highlight, and make notes in the book as you read through the chapters. We never stop learning, so let the journey begin.

Chapter 1

A BETTER YOU

Wnial school and by reading how-to books, so we can better
ourselves in certain areas. From this we hope to increase our salary, to
get a promotion, or to have the satisfaction that we are able to reach a
goal.

Why not improve the *inside* of us so it will radiate love, forgiveness,
peace, patience, faith, goodness, and many other righteous qualities?
We will be a magnet for blessings, love, courage, comfort, and wisdom.
Sign up for God's school by reading the Bible!

> "Within the covers of the Bible are the answers for all the
> problems men face."
> —President Ronald Reagan

These verses from the Bible will help you become a better you:

"You will show me the path of life; in Your presence is fullness of joy; at
Your right hand are pleasures forevermore" (Psalm 16:11 NKJV).

"Commit your works to the Lord, and your thoughts will be established" (Proverbs 16:3 NKJV).

"He who is slow to anger is better than the mighty, and he who rules his spirit than he who takes a city" (Proverbs 16:32 NKJV).

"He answered, 'While the child was still alive, I fasted and wept. I thought, "Who knows? The Lord may be gracious to me and let the child live." But now that he is dead, why should I fast? Can I bring him back again? I will go to him, but he will not return to me'" (2 Samuel 12:22–23 NIV).

"The beginning of strife is like letting out water, so quit before the quarrel breaks out" (Proverbs 17:14 ESV).

"He who gives an answer before he hears, it is folly and shame to him" (Proverbs 18:13 NASB). Note: *Folly* is a lack of good sense, understanding, or foresight.

"A good name is to be more desired than great wealth, favor is better than silver and gold" (Proverbs 22:1 NASB).

"Kick out the troublemakers and things will quiet down; you need a break from bickering and griping!" (Proverbs 22:10 MSG).

"Make no friendship with an angry man, and with a furious man do not go, lest you learn his ways and set a snare for your soul" (Proverbs 22:24–25 NKJV).

"Do not rejoice when your enemy falls, and do not let your heart be glad when he stumbles" (Proverbs 24:17 NKJV).

"Do not bring hastily to court, for what will you do in the end if your neighbor puts you to shame? If you argue your case with a neighbor, do not betray another man's confidence, or he who hears it may shame you and you will never lose your bad reputation" (Proverbs 25:8–10 NIV).

"Whatever your hand finds to do, do it with your might" (Ecclesiastes 9:10 NKJV).

"So let us know, let us press on to know the Lord. His going forth is as certain as the dawn; and He will come to us like the rain, like the spring rain watering the earth" (Hosea 6:3 NASB).

"Let your foot rarely be in your neighbor's house, or he will become weary of you and hate you" (Proverbs 25:17 NASB).

"Return to the LORD your God, for He is gracious and merciful, slow to anger, and of great kindness; and He relents from doing harm" (Joel 2:13 NKJV).

"Be still, and know that I am God; I will be exalted among the nations, I will be exalted in the earth!" (Psalm 46:10 NKJV).

"The person who belongs to God accepts what God says. But you don't accept what God says, because you don't belong to God" (John 8:47 NCV).

"You then who teach others, do you not teach yourself? While you preach against stealing, do you steal? You who say that one must not commit adultery, do you commit adultery?" (Romans 2:21–22 ESV).

"And do not be conformed to this world, but be transformed by the renewing of your mind, that you may prove what is that good and acceptable and perfect will of God" (Romans 12:2 NKJV).

"Rejoice with those who rejoice, and weep with those who weep" (Romans 12:15 NKJV).

"Repay no one evil for evil. Have regard for good things in the sight of all men. If it is possible, as much as depends on you, live peaceably with all men" (Romans 12:17–18 NKJV).

"For the kingdom of God is not a matter of eating and drinking but of righteousness and peace and joy in the Holy Spirit. Whoever thus serves Christ is acceptable to God and approved by men. So then let us pursue what makes for peace and for mutual upbuilding" (Romans 14:17–19 ESV).

"All things are lawful, but not all things are profitable. All things are lawful, but not all things edify. Let no one seek his own good, but that of his neighbor" (1 Corinthians 10:23–24 NASB). Note: *Neighbor* means "fellowman."

"Therefore, if anyone is in Christ, he is a new creation; old things have passed away; behold, all things have become new. Now all things are of God, who has reconciled us to Himself through Jesus Christ" (2 Corinthians 5:17–18 NKJV).

"If you think you are too important to help someone, you are only fooling yourself. You are not that important. Pay careful attention to your own work, for then you will get the satisfaction of a job well done, and you won't need to compare yourself to anyone else. For we are each responsible for our own conduct" (Galatians 6:3–5 NLT).

"Therefore, laying aside falsehood, speak truth each one of you with his neighbor, for we are members of one another. Be angry, and yet do not sin; do not let the sun go down on your anger, and do not give the devil an opportunity. He who steals must steal no longer; but rather he must labor, performing with his own hands what is good, so that he will have something to share with one who has need. Let no unwholesome word proceed from your mouth, but only such a word as is good for edification according to the need of the moment, so that it will give grace to those who hear" (Ephesians 4:25–29 NASB).

"Let nothing be done through selfish ambition or conceit, but in lowliness of mind let each esteem others better than himself. Let each of you look out not only for his own interests, but also for the interests of others" (Philippians 2:3–4 NKJV).

"Forgetting those things which are behind and reaching forward to those things which are ahead" (Philippians 3:13 NKJV).

"Open my eyes, that I may behold wondrous things out of Your law" (Psalm 119:18 AMP).

"Turn away my eyes from looking at worthless things, and revive me in Your way" (Psalm 119:37 NKJV).

"Teach me good judgment, wise and right discernment, and knowledge, for I have believed (trusted, relied on, and clung to) Your commandments" (Psalm 119:66 AMP).

"Finally, brethren, whatever is true, whatever is honorable, whatever is right, whatever is pure, whatever is lovely, whatever is of good repute, if there is any excellence and if anything worthy of praise, dwell on these things" (Philippians 4:8 NASB).

"Rejoice always, pray without ceasing, in everything give thanks; for this is the will of God in Christ Jesus for you" (1 Thessalonians 5:16–18 NKJV).

"But godliness with contentment is great gain" (1 Timothy 6:6 NIV).

"And having food and clothing, with these we shall be content" (1 Timothy 6:8 NKJV).

"Pursue righteousness, godliness, faith, love, patience, gentleness" (1 Timothy 6:11 NKJV).

"Similarly, if anyone competes as an athlete, he does not receive the victor's crown unless he competes according to the rules" (2 Timothy 2:5 NIV).

"To speak evil of no one, to be peaceable, gentle, showing all humility to all men" (Titus 3:2 NKJV).

"But avoid foolish controversies and genealogies and arguments and quarrels about the law, because these are unprofitable and useless" (Titus 3:9 NIV).

"I long for Your salvation, O LORD, and Your law is my delight" (Psalm 119:174 NASB).

"Let us throw off everything that hinders and the sin that so easily entangles, and let us run with perseverance the race marked out for us. Let us fix our eyes on Jesus, the author and perfecter of our faith" (Hebrews 12:1–2 NIV).

"Make sure that your character is free from the love of money, being content with what you have" (Hebrews 13:5 NASB).

"Now the God of peace, who brought up from the dead the great Shepherd of the sheep through the blood of the eternal covenant, even Jesus our Lord, equip you in every good thing to do His will, working in us that which is pleasing in His sight, through Jesus Christ, to whom be the glory forever and ever. Amen" (Hebrews 13:20–21 NASB).

"Religion that God our Father accepts as pure and faultless is this: to look after orphans and widows in their distress and to keep oneself from being polluted by the world" (James 1:27 NIV).

"Finally, all of you be of one mind, having compassion for one another; love as brothers, be tenderhearted, be courteous; not returning evil for evil or reviling for reviling, but on the contrary blessing, knowing that you were called to this, that you may inherit a blessing. For 'He who would love life and see good days, let him refrain his tongue from evil, and his lips from speaking deceit. Let him turn away from evil and do good; let him seek peace and pursue it. For the eyes of the LORD are on the righteous, and His ears are open to their prayers; but the face of the LORD is against those who do evil'" (1 Peter 3:8–12 NKJV).

"Search me, O God, and know my heart; try me, and know my anxieties; and see if there is any wicked way in me, and lead me in the way everlasting" (Psalm 139:23–24 NKJV).

"Be hospitable to one another without grumbling" (1 Peter 4:9 NKJV).

"Add to your faith virtue, to virtue knowledge, to knowledge self-control, to self-control perseverance, to perseverance godliness, to godliness brotherly kindness, and to brotherly kindness love. For if these things are yours and abound, you will be neither barren nor unfruitful in the knowledge of our Lord Jesus Christ" (2 Peter 1:5–8 NKJV).

"Cause me to hear Your loving-kindness in the morning, for on You do I lean and in You do I trust. Cause me to know the way wherein I should walk, for I lift up my inner self to You. Deliver me, O LORD, from my enemies; I flee to You to hide me. Teach me to do Your will, for You are my God; let Your good Spirit lead me into a level country and into the land of uprightness. Save my life, O LORD, for Your name's sake; in Your righteousness, bring my life out of trouble and free me from distress. And in your mercy and loving-kindness, cut off my enemies and destroy all those who afflict my inner self, for I am Your servant" (Psalm 143:8–12 AMP).

Chapter 2

ABIDE IN ME

When you are aware of God's presence,
you are able to see things from God's perspective.
—Dr. Charles Stanley

When you have a big project to tackle, isn't it easier to have another person's help to achieve your objective?

This book was a big project, and I remember saying to a friend, "What have I gotten myself into?" But as soon as that thought left my mouth, I knew why I was doing it, and I knew God was my partner in this venture. God inspired me with thoughts and drew me closer to Him as I read His Word.

The more God is part of you, the better your life is. As Oswald Chambers said in his book *My Utmost for His Highest*, "Be obsessed by God."

These verses will help you stay close to God and to abide (rest and dwell) in Him:

"Therefore say to them, 'Thus says the LORD of hosts: "Return to Me,"' says the LORD of hosts, "and I will return to you," says the LORD of hosts'" (Zechariah 1:3 NKJV).

"Abide in Me, and I in you. As the branch cannot bear fruit of itself, unless it abides in the vine, neither can you, unless you abide in Me. I am the vine, you are the branches. He who abides in Me, and I in him, bears much fruit; for without Me you can do nothing. If anyone does not abide in Me, he is cast out as a branch and is withered; and they gather them and throw them into the fire, and they are burned. If you abide in Me, and My words abide in you, you will ask what you desire, and it shall be done for you" (John 15:4–7 NKJV).

"Test yourselves to see if you are in the faith; examine yourselves! Or do you not recognize this about yourselves, that Jesus Christ is in you" (2 Corinthians 13:5 NASB).

"It is no longer I who live, but Christ lives in me; and the life which I now live in the flesh I live by faith in the Son of God, who loved me and gave Himself for me" (Galatians 2:20 NKJV).

"Therefore submit to God. Resist the devil and he will flee from you. Draw near to God and He will draw near to you" (James 4:7–8 NKJV).

"The one who keeps His commandments abides in Him, and He in him. We know by this that He abides in us, by the Spirit whom He has given us" (1 John 3:24 NASB).

"You are from God. . . . because greater is He who is in you than he who is in the world" (1 John 4:4 NASB).

"By this we come to know (perceive, recognize, and understand) that we abide (live and remain) in Him and He in us: because He has given (imparted) to us of His [Holy] Spirit" (1 John 4:13 AMP).

"And we have known and believed the love that God has for us. God is love, and he who abides in love abides in God, and God in him" (1 John 4:16 NKJV).

Chapter 3

ADULTERY—AFFAIR

The late Dr. D. James Kennedy said that if you want to change opinion about a subject, you have to change the language.

That is exactly what happened in the late 1960s. The word *adultery* was replaced by the word *affair*. *Adultery* conjures up a disquieting feeling, while *affair*, on the other hand, sounds harmless. In *Webster's Unabridged Dictionary* under *affair*, the last definition reads: "[from love affair] an amorous relationship or episode between two people not married to each other; an amour." You will note that there is no specific reference to adultery or that a married person is involved. The two people could be single.

The other night on Turner Classic Movies, I happened upon the last half of *A Ticklish Affair*, which was produced in 1963. Immediately I thought that one of the characters was cheating on his wife or husband, since I knew nothing about the movie. The plot involved a widow and a single man who had fallen in love, resulting in complications. But there was no adultery. In the early 1960s, *affair* did not mean adultery.

You can change the word all you want, but adultery is adultery. God is not tricked.

"Whoever commits adultery with a woman lacks understanding; he who does so destroys his own soul" (Proverbs 6:32 NKJV).

"My son, keep my words, and treasure my commands within you. Keep my commands and live, and my law as the apple of your eye. Bind them on your fingers; write them on the tablet of your heart. Say to wisdom, 'You are my sister,' and call understanding your nearest kin, that they may keep you from the immoral woman, from the seductress who flatters with her words" (Proverbs 7:1–5 NKJV).

"'I have perfumed my bed with myrrh, aloes and cinnamon. Come, let's drink deep of love till morning; let's enjoy ourselves with love! My husband is not at home; he has gone on a long journey. He took his purse filled with money and will not be home till full moon.' With persuasive words she led him astray; she seduced him with her smooth talk. All at once he followed her like an ox going to the slaughter, like a deer stepping into a noose till an arrow pierces his liver, like a bird darting into a snare, little knowing it will cost him his life" (Proverbs 7:17–23 NIV).

"For a harlot is a deep pit and an adulterous woman is a narrow well. Surely she lurks as a robber, and increases the faithless among men" (Proverbs 23:27–28 NASB).

"This is the way of an adulteress: She eats and wipes her mouth and says, 'I've done nothing wrong'" (Proverbs 30:20 NIV).

Chapter 4

ASKING AND RECEIVING

Do you remember when you asked your parents for that can't-live-without-it sweater, or maybe a car? And do you remember their answer? "No!" We may be asking God for something too and not getting the response we want.

When you tell God, "I want _____," be specific about what you are asking for, ask it in Jesus' name, have faith, and obey God's laws. If you do not receive your request, God will give you something better because He *knows* what is *best* for you! Believe.

"Ask, and it will be given to you; seek, and you will find; knock, and it will be opened to you. For everyone who asks receives, and he who seeks finds, and to him who knocks it will be opened. Or what man is there among you who, if his son asks for bread, will give him a stone? Or if he asks for a fish, will he give him a serpent? If you then, being evil, know how to give good gifts to your children, how much more will your Father who is in heaven give good things to those who ask Him!" (Matthew 7:7–11 NKJV).

"So I say to you: Ask and it will be given to you; seek and you will find; knock and the door will be opened to you. For everyone who asks receives; he who seeks finds; and to him who knocks, the door will be opened" (Luke 11:9–10 NIV).

"Truly, truly, I say to you, if you ask the Father for anything in My name, He will give it to you. Until now you have asked for nothing in My name; ask and you will receive, so that your joy may be made full" (John 16:23–24 NASB).

"And whatever we ask we receive from Him, because we keep His commandments and do those things that are pleasing in His sight" (1 John 3:22 NKJV).

"And this is the confidence (the assurance, the privilege of boldness) which we have in Him: [we are sure] that if we ask anything (make any request) according to His will (in agreement with His own plan), He listens to and hears us" (1 John 5:14 AMP).

Chapter 5

BLESS, BLESSINGS, AND BLESSED

If you're worried and you can't sleep,
Just count your blessings instead of sheep.
—Irving Berlin

In your ever overactive and overfilled days, you forget how blessed you are, especially when the boss reprimands you, or you lock yourself out of the car, or you are late for an important meeting, or you just found out that you need a dozen cookies for a meeting in two hours! Blessed?

How do you know that the frustrating incidents in your life aren't really beneficial in some way? The boss's reprimand may in the long run help you make better decisions, the locked car that you can't get into might have prevented you from being involved in an accident, and the dozen cookies could have given you the opportunity to find a wonderful bakery. Honestly, you may never know what blessings you have derived from your so-called catastrophes.

You *do* know your obvious blessings, like a roof over your head, food to eat, friends, and the fact that God loves you. How much more blessed can you be? The best blessing of all is that God loves *you*!

"He will bless you if you obey the LORD your God completely, but you must be careful to obey all the commands I am giving you today. The LORD your God will bless you as he promised" (Deuteronomy 15:5–6 NCV).

"Blessed is the nation whose God is the LORD" (Psalm 33:12 NASB).

"Blessed is the man who makes the LORD his trust, who does not look to the proud, to those who turn aside to false gods" (Psalm 40:4 NIV).

"Blessings crown the head of the righteous" (Proverbs 10:6 NIV).

"It is the blessing of the LORD that makes rich, and He adds no sorrow to it" (Proverbs 10:22 NASB).

"Blessed is the man whom God corrects; so do not despise the discipline of the Almighty" (Job 5:17 NIV).

"Thus says the LORD: 'Keep justice, and do righteousness. . . . Blessed is the man who does this, . . . who keeps from defiling the Sabbath, and keeps his hand from doing any evil'" (Isaiah 56:1–2 NKJV).

"People curse the man who hoards grain, but blessing crowns him who is willing to sell" (Proverbs 11:26 NIV).

"Blessed are the people who know the joyful sound! They walk, O LORD, in the light of Your countenance" (Psalm 89:15 NKJV).

"Blessed is the man whom You instruct, O LORD, and teach out of Your law" (Psalm 94:12 NKJV).

"Blessed are those who keep justice, and he who does righteousness at all times!" (Psalm 106:3 NKJV).

"Blessed is the man who trusts in the LORD, and whose hope is the LORD. For he shall be like a tree planted by the waters, which spreads out its roots by the river, and will not fear when heat comes; but its leaf will be green, and will not be anxious in the year of drought, nor will cease from yielding fruit" (Jeremiah 17:7–8 NKJV).

"Blessed is he who is kind to the needy" (Proverbs 14:21 NIV).

"A faithful man will be richly blessed, but one eager to get rich will not go unpunished" (Proverbs 28:20 NIV).

"Blessed (happy, fortunate, to be envied) is everyone who fears, reveres, and worships the LORD, who walks in His ways and lives according to His commandments" (Psalm 128:1 AMP).

"Behold, thus shall the man be blessed who reverently and worshipfully fears the LORD" (Psalm 128:4 AMP).

"And blessed is he who is not offended because of Me" (Luke 7:23 NKJV).

"But He said, 'More than that, blessed are those who hear the word of God and keep it!'" (Luke 11:28 NKJV).

"Truly, truly, I say to you, a slave is not greater than his master, nor is one who is sent greater than the one who sent him. If you know these things, you are blessed if you do them" (John 13:16–17 NASB).

"Jesus said to him, 'Thomas, because you have seen Me, you have believed. Blessed are those who have not seen and yet have believed'" (John 20:29 NKJV).

"Bless those who persecute you; bless and do not curse" (Romans 12:14 NIV).

"Blessed is the man who endures temptation; for when he has been approved, he will receive the crown of life which the Lord has promised to those who love Him" (James 1:12 NKJV).

"As you know, we consider blessed those who have persevered. You have heard of Job's perseverance and have seen what the Lord finally brought about. The Lord is full of compassion and mercy" (James 5:11 NIV).

"But even if you should suffer for righteousness' sake, you are blessed" (1 Peter 3:14 NKJV).

Chapter 6

COMFORT

When a child has fallen and scratched his knee, he runs and cries for his mother. Tenderly the mother comforts her child by cleaning and putting antiseptic on the scratch, taking her child in her arms, holding him, and wiping away his tears.

When God is in your life, that is exactly how you'll feel. His arms will wrap around you, giving you comfort in every disastrous moment. Be comforted by reading God's Word. "The LORD is my shepherd; I shall not want" (Psalm 23:1 NKJV).

"Blessed be the God and Father of our Lord Jesus Christ, the Father of mercies and God of all comfort, who comforts us in all our tribulation, that we may be able to comfort those who are in any trouble, with the comfort with which we ourselves are comforted by God" (2 Corinthians 1:3–4 NKJV).

"Now may our Lord Jesus Christ Himself and God our Father, who has loved us and given us eternal comfort and good hope by grace, comfort and strengthen your hearts in every good work and word" (2 Thessalonians 2:16–17 NASB).

"In the multitude of my anxieties within me, Your comforts delight my soul" (Psalm 94:19 NKJV).

"This is my comfort and consolation in my affliction: that Your word has revived me and given me life" (Psalm 119:50 AMP).

Chapter 7

CREATION—EARTH AND YOU

If you ask high school students whether they believe in creationism or evolution, you probably will find most students saying they believe in evolution. This is because most public schools teach evolution and nothing or very little about creationism.

Michael Berkman, a political scientist at Pennsylvania State University, did research on a random sampling of two thousand high-school science teachers throughout the United States in 2007. In the 939 responses, 2 percent of teachers said that they did not cover evolution, while the majority spent between three and ten classroom hours on this subject. It is interesting to note that a quarter of the teachers said that they did spend some time teaching creationism or intelligent design.[1]

The Institute for Creation Research is nearly forty years old. Its studies scientifically reveal the fallacies of evolution and show evidence supporting intelligent design by the Creator.

It is time that there is a fair and balanced teaching of facts on creationism and evolution in the classroom. Truth should not be stifled in our schools.

"And He answered and said to them, 'Have you not read that He who made them at the beginning "made them male and female"?'" (Matthew 19:4 NKJV).

"In the beginning was the Word, and the Word was with God, and the Word was God. He was in the beginning with God. All things were made through Him, and without Him nothing was made that was made. In Him was life, and the life was the light of men" (John 1:1–4 NKJV).

"God, who made the world and everything in it, since He is Lord of heaven and earth, does not dwell in temples made with hands. Nor is He worshiped with men's hands, as though He needed anything, since He gives to all life, breath, and all things. And He has made from one blood every nation of men to dwell on all the face of the earth, and has determined their preappointed times and the boundaries of their dwellings, so that they should seek the Lord, in the hope that they might grope for Him and find Him, though He is not far from each one of us; for in Him we live and move and have our being, as also some of your own poets have said, 'For we are also His offspring'" (Acts 17:24–28 NKJV).

"Yours is the day, Yours also is the night; You have prepared the light and the sun. You have established all the boundaries of the earth; You have made summer and winter" (Psalm 74:16–17 NASB).

"For the LORD is the great God, and the great King above all gods. In His hand are the deep places of the earth; the heights of the hills are His also. The sea is His, for He made it; and His hands formed the dry land" (Psalm 95:3–5 NKJV).

"The rich and the poor have a common bond, the LORD is the maker of them all" (Proverbs 22:2 NASB).

"For every house is built by someone, but the builder of all things is God" (Hebrews 3:4 NASB).

"Worthy are You, our Lord and our God, to receive glory and honor and power; for You created all things, and because of Your will they existed, and were created" (Revelation 4:11 NASB).

"For you formed my inward parts; you knitted me together in my mother's womb. I praise you, for I am fearfully and wonderfully made. Wonderful are your works; my soul knows it very well. My frame was not hidden from you, when I was being made in secret, intricately woven in the depths of the earth. Your eyes saw my unformed substance; in your book were written, every one of them, the days that were formed for me, when as yet there was none of them" (Psalm 139:13–16 ESV).

Chapter 8

DO NOT BE AFRAID

A man's life is what his thoughts make of it.
—Marcus Aurelius

Too many times in our lives, we become fearful of getting sick, losing a job, not having enough money, not being able to accomplish goals, and on and on. The fear becomes so real that it becomes a reality.

When a fearful thought arises, say, "Stop!" Reverse that negative thought to a positive outcome. Visualize it and believe it. Affirm it through affirmations. Affirmations are positive statements that we repeat throughout the day. Our affirmations can be verses from the Bible or our own positive statements. Write them on cards and place them where you can see them. You may want to place the card on the bathroom mirror, on the dashboard of the car, or on your desk at work. Doing all three—visualizing, believing, and affirming—will take away your fear.

I remember being afraid to fly. I knew I had to overcome this fear, so I visualized myself being seated in a plane. I felt all of the anxiety as if I were on the plane. My stomach was upset, I was sweaty, and I thought everyone on the plane was watching me. I realized I felt this way because I was claustrophobic. I did this visualizing exercise day after day, feeling all of the anxiety, but also during the visualizing exercise I gave myself a positive self-talk and visualized my flight. I told myself the following:

- I could get out of my seat and walk in the aisle.
- The other passengers weren't watching me, but were doing other things.
- It was a time to relax, take deep breaths, and enjoy the trip.
- God was with me.

Every day the anxiety decreased, until finally I could visualize flying on a plane as a pleasant experience. I can now fly without being fearful.

By the way, when you are in a frightening situation, it helps to visualize Jesus beside you and protecting you.

"You will not fear the terror of night, nor the arrow that flies by day" (Psalm 91:5 NIV).

"Be not afraid of sudden terror and panic, nor of the stormy blast or the storm and ruin of the wicked when it comes [for you will be guiltless], for the LORD shall be your confidence, firm and strong, and shall keep your foot from being caught [in a trap or some hidden danger]" (Proverbs 3:25–26 AMP).

"And Moses said to the people, 'Do not be afraid. Stand still, and see the salvation of the LORD, which He will accomplish for you today. For the Egyptians whom you see today, you shall see again no more forever. The LORD will fight for you, and you shall hold your peace'" (Exodus 14:13–14 NKJV).

"When you go out to war against your enemies, and see horses and chariots and an army larger than your own, you shall not be afraid of them, for the LORD your God is with you" (Deuteronomy 20:1 ESV).

"And he shall say to them, 'Hear, O Israel: Today you are on the verge of battle with your enemies. Do not let your heart faint, do not be afraid, and do not tremble or be terrified because of them; for the

LORD your God is He who goes with you, to fight for you against your enemies, to save you'" (Deuteronomy 20:3–4 NKJV).

"Be strong and of good courage, do not fear nor be afraid of them; for the LORD your God, He is the One who goes with you. He will not leave you nor forsake you" (Deuteronomy 31:6 NKJV).

"Have I not commanded you? Be strong and of good courage; do not be afraid, nor be dismayed, for the LORD your God is with you wherever you go" (Joshua 1:9 NKJV).

"Joshua said to them, Fear not nor be dismayed; be strong and of good courage. For thus shall the LORD do to all your enemies against whom you fight" (Joshua 10:25 AMP).

"But she said, 'As the LORD your God lives, I have no bread, only a handful of flour in the bowl and a little oil in the jar; and behold, I am gathering a few sticks that I may go in and prepare for me and my son, that we may eat it and die.' Then Elijah said to her, 'Do not fear; go, do as you have said, but make me a little bread cake from it first and bring it out to me, and afterward you may make one for yourself and for your son. For thus says the LORD God of Israel, "The bowl of flour shall not be exhausted, nor shall the jar of oil be empty, until the day that the LORD sends rain on the face of the earth."' So she went and did according to the word of Elijah, and she and he and her household ate for many days. The bowl of flour was not exhausted nor did the jar of oil become empty, according to the word of the LORD which He spoke through Elijah" (1 Kings 17:12–16 NASB). Note: Elijah was a Hebrew prophet of the ninth century BC.

"The LORD says this to you: Be not afraid or dismayed at this great multitude; for the battle is not yours, but God's" (2 Chronicles 20:15 AMP).

"'Be strong and courageous. Do not be afraid or discouraged because of the king of Assyria and the vast army with him, for there is a greater power with us than with him. With him is only the arm of flesh, but with us is the LORD our God to help us and to fight our battles.' And the people gained confidence from what Hezekiah the king of Judah said" (2 Chronicles 32:7–8 NIV). Note: You will find later on in this chapter that Hezekiah won the battle against the king of Assyria with God's help.

"What I feared has come upon me; what I dreaded has happened to me" (Job 3:25 NIV).

"With this news, strengthen those who have tired hands, and encourage those who have weak knees. Say to those with fearful hearts, 'Be strong, and do not fear, for your God is coming to destroy your enemies. He is coming to save you'" (Isaiah 35:3–4 NLT).

"Fear not, for I am with you; be not dismayed, for I am your God. I will strengthen you, yes, I will help you, I will uphold you with My righteous right hand" (Isaiah 41:10 NKJV).

"For I, the LORD your God, will hold your right hand, saying to you, 'Fear not, I will help you'" (Isaiah 41:13 NKJV).

"But immediately Jesus spoke to them, saying, 'Take courage, it is I; do not be afraid'" (Matthew 14:27 NASB).

"As soon as Jesus heard the word that was spoken, He said to the ruler of the synagogue, 'Do not be afraid; only believe'" (Mark 5:36 NKJV).

"The LORD is on my side; I will not fear. What can man do to me?" (Psalm 118:6 NKJV).

Chapter 9

ETERNAL LIFE—
TO LIVE FOREVER

Have you heard someone say, "I wish I could live forever!"? The good news is, you can! If you believe in Jesus, you will have an eternal home in heaven.

My father died suddenly at a young age. I was not prepared for this, but I am so thankful that my dad was. He had accepted Jesus in his life and now has an eternal home with God. That is what made his death bearable. He is gone from his earthly life, but I will be reunited with him in God's kingdom. I will see my dad again.

If you know of someone who does not know Jesus, please introduce him to Jesus. We can't make a person know Jesus, but we can give him the opportunity. The choice will then be up to him.

As you read the following Bible verses, you will see other words referring to eternal life, such as *live, life, living, never die,* and *saved.*

"For You have delivered my soul from death, indeed my feet from stumbling, so that I may walk before God in the light of the living" (Psalm 56:13 NASB).

"The fears of the wicked will be fulfilled; the hopes of the godly will be granted. When the storms of life come, the wicked are whirled away, but the godly have a lasting foundation" (Proverbs 10:24–25 NLT).

"Who has walked in My statutes and kept My ordinances, to deal justly; [then] he is [truly] righteous; he shall surely live, says the LORD God" (Ezekiel 18:9 AMP).

"'For I have no pleasure in the death of anyone who dies,' declares the Lord GOD. 'Therefore, repent and live'" (Ezekiel 18:32 NASB).

"And it shall come to pass that whoever calls on the name of the LORD shall be saved" (Joel 2:32 NKJV).

"For the Son of Man has come to save that which was lost" (Matthew 18:11 NKJV). Note: Jesus was referred to as the *Son of Man.*

"I will never forget your commandments, for by them you give me life" (Psalm 119:93 NLT).

"Now as He was going out on the road, one came running, knelt before Him, and asked Him, 'Good Teacher, what shall I do that I may inherit eternal life?' So Jesus said to him, 'Why do you call Me good? No one is good but One, that is, God. You know the commandments: "Do not commit adultery," "Do not murder," "Do not steal," "Do not bear false witness," "Do not defraud," "Honor your father and your mother."' And he answered and said to Him, 'Teacher, all these things I have kept from my youth.' Then Jesus, looking at him, loved him, and said to him, 'One thing you lack: Go your way, sell whatever you have and give to the poor, and you will have treasure in heaven; and come, take up the cross, and follow Me'" (Mark 10:17–21 NKJV).

"Whoever believes and is baptized will be saved, but whoever does not believe will be condemned" (Mark 16:16 NIV). Note: Jesus is speaking.

"Whoever believes in Him should not perish but have eternal life. For God so loved the world that He gave His only begotten Son, that whoever believes in Him should not perish but have everlasting life" (John 3:15–16 NKJV).

"The Father loves the Son and has placed everything in his hands. Whoever believes in the Son has eternal life, but whoever rejects the Son will not see life, for God's wrath remains on him" (John 3:35–36 NIV).

"I assure you, most solemnly I tell you, the person whose ears are open to My words [who listens to My message] and believes and trusts in and clings to and relies on Him who sent Me has (possesses now) eternal life. And he does not come into judgment [does not incur sentence of judgment, will not come under condemnation], but he has already passed over out of death into life. Believe Me when I assure you, most solemnly I tell you, the time is coming and is here now when the dead shall hear the voice of the Son of God and those who hear it shall live" (John 5:24–25 AMP).

"You are unwilling to come to Me so that you may have life" (John 5:40 NASB). Note: Jesus is speaking.

"And Jesus said to them, 'I am the bread of life. He who comes to Me shall never hunger, and he who believes in Me shall never thirst'" (John 6:35 NKJV).

"As the living Father sent Me, and I live because of the Father, so he who feeds on Me will live because of Me" (John 6:57 NKJV).

"My sheep hear My voice, and I know them, and they follow Me; and I give eternal life to them, and they will never perish; and no one will snatch them out of My hand. My Father, who has given them to Me, is greater than all; and no one is able to snatch them out of the Father's hand" (John 10:27–29 NASB).

"Jesus said to her, 'I am the resurrection and the life; he who believes in Me will live even if he dies, and everyone who lives and believes in Me will never die'" (John 11:25–26 NASB).

"The man who loves his life will lose it, while the man who hates his life in this world will keep it for eternal life" (John 12:25 NIV).

"But now that you have been set free from sin and have become slaves to God, the benefit you reap leads to holiness, and the result is eternal life. For the wages of sin is death, but the gift of God is eternal life in Christ Jesus our Lord" (Romans 6:22–23 NIV).

"For the things which are seen are temporary, but the things which are not seen are eternal" (2 Corinthians 4:18 NKJV).

"For we know that if our earthly house, this tent, is destroyed, we have a building from God, a house not made with hands, eternal in the heavens" (2 Corinthians 5:1 NKJV).

"A faith and knowledge resting on the hope of eternal life, which God, who does not lie, promised before the beginning of time" (Titus 1:2 NIV).

"And this is the promise that He has promised us—eternal life" (1 John 2:25 NKJV).

EVIL

When we think of evil, most people think of the devil. That's the man in the red suit with pointy ears and a tail, holding a pitchfork in his hand.

Aside from the fictional character, the devil (*d* for *damnation* plus *evil*) can appear as a well-dressed man, a voluptuous woman, a disheveled boy, or an intellectual. No matter how the devil appears, he spews evil. His mission is to turn you away from God.

Hate evil! Evil is morally wrong. It only causes harm to you and others. Always be on guard, so you don't become ensnared by evil ways. How do you do that? You stay continually in touch with God through reading the Bible, talking with Him, and listening to what God tells you.

"He made his own son pass through fire. He practiced magic and told the future by explaining signs and dreams, and he got advice from mediums and fortune-tellers. He did many things the LORD said were wrong, which made the LORD angry" (2 Kings 21:6 NCV). Note: This passage is talking about King Manasseh in Jerusalem.

"A worthless man devises and digs up mischief, and in his lips there is as a scorching fire. A perverse man sows strife, and a whisperer separates close friends. The exceedingly grasping, covetous, and violent man entices his neighbor, leading him in a way that is not good. He who shuts his eyes to devise perverse things and who compresses his lips [as if in concealment] brings evil to pass" (Proverbs 16:27–30 AMP).

"The crooked heart will not prosper; the lying tongue tumbles into trouble" (Proverbs 17:20 NLT).

"For from within, out of the heart of men, proceed evil thoughts, adulteries, fornications, murders, thefts, covetousness, wickedness, deceit, lewdness, an evil eye, blasphemy, pride, foolishness. All these evil things come from within and defile a man" (Mark 7:21–23 NKJV).

"The world cannot [be expected to] hate you, but it does hate Me because I denounce it for its wicked works and reveal that its doings are evil" (John 7:7 AMP).

"Hate what is evil" (Romans 12:9 NIV).

"But if you do what is evil, be afraid" (Romans 13:4 NASB).

"Do not be envious of evil men, nor desire to be with them; for their heart devises violence, and their lips talk of troublemaking" (Proverbs 24:1–2 NKJV).

"Abstain from every form of evil" (1 Thessalonians 5:22 ESV).

"But those who want to get rich fall into temptation and a snare and many foolish and harmful desires which plunge men into ruin and destruction. For the love of money is a root of all sorts of evil, and some by longing for it have wandered away from the faith and pierced themselves with many griefs" (1 Timothy 6:9–10 NASB).

"Do not speak evil against one another, brothers" (James 4:11 ESV).

"As it is, you boast in your arrogance. All such boasting is evil" (James 4:16 ESV).

Chapter 11

FAITH

Do you remember telling a person something you were going to do, and his reply was, "Do you really think you can?" or "You can't do that. It's impossible!" When we hear negative comments like that, we may start to think, *Maybe I can't,* and our minds begin to fill with self-doubt. This is when we need faith.

Many times, outward appearances can shake our faith. You probably remember hearing "Seeing is believing," but faith says "Believing is seeing." Jesus said to his disciple Thomas, "Blessed are those who have not seen and yet have believed" (John 20:29 NKJV).

When we receive Jesus as our Savior, the Holy Spirit enters us. The Holy Spirit is a power source who will help generate faith and remind us "with God all things are possible" (Mark 10:27 NKJV).

"For she said to herself, 'If only I may touch His garment, I shall be made well.' But Jesus turned around, and when He saw her He said, 'Be of good cheer, daughter; your faith has made you well.' And the woman was made well from that hour" (Matthew 9:21–22 NKJV).

"Then Jesus answered her, 'O woman, great is your faith! Be it done for you as you desire.' And her daughter was healed instantly" (Matthew 15:28 ESV).

"This Good News tells us how God makes us right in his sight. This is accomplished from start to finish by faith. As the Scriptures say, 'It is through faith that a righteous person has life'" (Romans 1:17 NLT).

"Since we have been made right with God by our faith, we have peace with God. This happened through our Lord Jesus Christ, who through our faith has brought us into that blessing of God's grace that we now enjoy. And we are happy because of the hope we have of sharing God's glory" (Romans 5:1–2 NCV).

"But is now disclosed and through the prophetic Scriptures is made known to all nations, according to the command of the eternal God, [to win them] to obedience to the faith, to [the] only wise God be glory forevermore through Jesus Christ (the Anointed One)! Amen (so be it)" (Romans 16:26–27 AMP).

"Your faith should not be in the wisdom of men but in the power of God" (1 Corinthians 2:5 NKJV).

"For you stand firm in your faith" (2 Corinthians 1:24 ESV).

"For we walk by faith, not by sight" (2 Corinthians 5:7 ESV).

"Yet we know that a person is made right with God by faith in Jesus Christ, not by obeying the law. And we have believed in Christ Jesus, so that we might be made right with God because of our faith in Christ, not because we have obeyed the law. For no one will ever be made right with God by obeying the law" (Galatians 2:16 NLT).

"For you are all children of God through faith in Christ Jesus" (Galatians 3:26 NLT).

"This was in accordance with the eternal purpose which He carried out in Christ Jesus our Lord, in whom we have boldness and confident access through faith in Him" (Ephesians 3:11–12 NASB).

"I count all things to be loss in view of the surpassing value of knowing Christ Jesus my Lord, for whom I have suffered the loss of all things, and count them but rubbish so that I may gain Christ, and may be found in Him, not having a righteousness of my own derived from the Law, but that which is through faith in Christ, the righteousness which comes from God on the basis of faith" (Philippians 3:8–9 NASB).

"I have fought the good fight, I have finished the race, I have kept the faith" (2 Timothy 4:7 NKJV). Note: The apostle Paul stated this.

"We do not want you to become lazy, but to imitate those who through faith and patience inherit what has been promised" (Hebrews 6:12 NIV).

"Now faith is the substance of things hoped for, the evidence of things not seen" (Hebrews 11:1 NKJV).

"And without faith it is impossible to please Him, for he who comes to God must believe that He is and that He is a rewarder of those who seek Him" (Hebrews 11:6 NASB).

"By faith Noah, being warned by God about things not yet seen, in reverence prepared an ark for the salvation of his household, by which he condemned the world, and became an heir of the righteousness which is according to faith. By faith Abraham, when he was called, obeyed by going out to a place which he was to receive for an inheritance; and he went out, not knowing where he was going. By faith he lived as an alien in the land of promise, as in a foreign land, dwelling in tents with Isaac and Jacob, fellow heirs of the same promise; for he was looking for the city which has foundations, whose architect and builder is God. By faith even Sarah herself received ability to conceive, even beyond the proper time of life, since she considered Him faithful who had promised" (Hebrews 11:7–11 NASB).

"By faith Moses, when he had grown up, refused to be known as the son of Pharaoh's daughter. He chose to be mistreated along with the people of God rather than to enjoy the pleasures of sin for a short time. He regarded disgrace for the sake of Christ as of greater value than the treasures of Egypt, because he was looking ahead to his reward" (Hebrews 11:24–26 NIV).

"If any of you lacks wisdom, let him ask God, who gives generously to all without reproach, and it will be given him. But let him ask in faith, with no doubting, for the one who doubts is like a wave of the sea that is driven and tossed by the wind" (James 1:5–6 ESV).

"For everyone who has been born of God overcomes the world. And this is the victory that has overcome the world—our faith" (1 John 5:4 ESV).

Chapter 12

FALSE PROPHETS

Satan (another name for the devil) is the father of lies. He is thrilled when he can trick people into believing lies. Satan is the master of making lies sound good and righteous.

As I mentioned in the introduction, the Bible is God's inspired Word. God has revealed to us His thoughts, actions, and ways through the men and women in His Bible and has warned us about false prophets. It is the Christian belief that the Bible is a "closed canon." This means that nothing more can be added to or subtracted from God's Word.

If you are undecided about whether what someone purporting to be a prophet says is true, seek God's wisdom through His Word. Objectively look at this so-called prophet *without* emotional attachments. The decision must be based on God's truth and not on a feeling. A false prophet is one whose beliefs are *not* the same as God's Word, the Bible. Armor yourself in truth, not emotion.

"For such men are false apostles, deceitful workmen, disguising themselves as apostles of Christ. And no wonder, for even Satan disguises himself as an angel of light. So it is no surprise if his servants, also, disguise themselves as servants of righteousness. Their end will correspond to their deeds" (2 Corinthians 11:13–15 ESV).

"Evidently some people are throwing you into confusion and are trying to pervert the gospel of Christ. But even if we or an angel from heaven should preach a gospel other than the one we preached to you, let him be eternally condemned! As we have already said, so now I say again: If anybody is preaching to you a gospel other than what you accepted, let him be eternally condemned! Am I now trying to win the approval of men, or of God? Or am I trying to please men? If I were still trying to please men, I would not be a servant of Christ. I want you to know, brothers, that the gospel I preached is not something that man made up. I did not receive it from any man, nor was I taught it; rather, I received it by revelation from Jesus Christ" (Galatians 1:7–12 NIV).

"Dear friends, do not believe every spirit, but test the spirits to see whether they are from God, because many false prophets have gone out into the world. This is how you can recognize the Spirit of God: Every spirit that acknowledges that Jesus Christ has come in the flesh is from God, but every spirit that does not acknowledge Jesus is not from God. This is the spirit of the antichrist, which you have heard is coming and even now is already in the world" (1 John 4:1–3 NIV).

Chapter 13

FEAR OF GOD

As I was growing up, *fear* meant to be afraid or frightened of someone or something. When I went to church, I heard the minister say, quoting a Bible passage, "Fear God." Naturally, I thought that I was supposed to be afraid of God. Many years later, as I was listening to a sermon, the minister clarified the word *fear* in the context of fearing God. He said that it designates a reverence and devotion to God. What a difference a definition makes!

If you are like I was, I hope you will read the following Bible passages in a whole different way. Revere God and do not be afraid of Him.

"Let all the earth fear the LORD; let all the inhabitants of the world stand in awe of Him. For He spoke, and it was done; He commanded, and it stood fast" (Psalm 33:8–9 NASB).

"All who fear the LORD will hate evil. Therefore, I hate pride and arrogance, corruption and perverse speech" (Proverbs 8:13 NLT).

"O fear the LORD, you His saints; for to those who fear Him there is no want" (Psalm 34:9 NASB).

"For the LORD your God dried up the waters of the Jordan before you until you had crossed over, as the LORD your God did to the Red Sea, which He dried up before us until we had crossed over, that all the peoples of the earth may know the hand of the LORD, that it is mighty, that you may fear the LORD your God forever" (Joshua 4:23–24 NKJV).

"He who walks in his uprightness fears the LORD, but he who is devious in his ways despises Him" (Proverbs 14:2 NASB).

"In the fear of the LORD there is strong confidence, and his children will have refuge. The fear of the LORD is a fountain of life, that one may avoid the snares of death" (Proverbs 14:26–27 NASB).

"Unfailing love and faithfulness make atonement for sin. By fearing the LORD, people avoid evil" (Proverbs 16:6 NLT).

"The fear of the LORD leads to life, and whoever has it rests satisfied; he will not be visited by harm" (Proverbs 19:23 ESV).

"Do not let your heart envy sinners, but be zealous for the fear of the LORD all the day" (Proverbs 23:17 NKJV).

"So great is His lovingkindness toward those who fear Him" (Psalm 103:11 NASB).

"Just as a father has compassion on his children, so the LORD has compassion on those who fear Him" (Psalm 103:13 NASB).

"The fear of the LORD is the beginning of wisdom; all those who practice it have a good understanding. His praise endures forever!" (Psalm 111:10 ESV).

"Fear the LORD, serve Him in sincerity and in truth" (Joshua 24:14 NKJV).

"Since we have these promises, beloved, let us cleanse ourselves from every defilement of body and spirit, bringing holiness to completion in the fear of God" (2 Corinthians 7:1 ESV).

"Charm is deceptive, and beauty does not last; but a woman who fears the LORD will be greatly praised" (Proverbs 31:30 NLT).

"Respect everyone, and love your Christian brothers and sisters. Fear God" (1 Peter 2:17 NLT).

Chapter 14

FOOL

Before we speak, do we take time to think through what we are going to say? Do we take time to research our positions or beliefs to make sure we are correct? "Lord, what fools these mortals be!" wrote William Shakespeare in *A Midsummer Night's Dream*.

Are you politically correct? By that I mean, do you say what is expected and not necessarily what you mean or believe, such as saying, "Happy Holidays" instead of "Merry Christmas." I used to be, because I didn't educate myself on the facts and because I wanted to fit in and not offend anyone. Offending people makes us look bad, especially if we are Christians. I want to make two points: First, politically *correct* is not politically *right*. Second, if we are Christians, followers of God's law, we do not lie. Whom are we trying to impress—man or God? Who is more important—man or God? But when the truth is being hidden, no matter whom it offends, we are dishonest and fools in God's eyes. Making points with men doesn't make points with God.

A children's story, *The Emperor's New Clothes* by Hans Christian Andersen, is a perfect example of political correctness. Here is a portion of the story:

The good old minister went into the room where the swindlers sat before the empty looms. "Heaven preserve us!" he thought, and opened his eyes wide, "I cannot see anything at all," but he did not say so. Both swindlers requested him to come near, and asked him if he did not admire the exquisite pattern and the beautiful colours, pointing to the empty looms. The poor old minister tried his very best, but he could see nothing, for there was nothing to be seen. "Oh dear," he thought, "can I be so stupid? I should never have thought so, and nobody must know it! Is it possible that I am not fit for my office? No, no, I cannot say that I was unable to see the cloth."

"Now, have you got nothing to say?" said one of the swindlers, while he pretended to be busily weaving.

"Oh, it is very pretty, exceedingly beautiful," replied the old minister looking through his glasses. "What a beautiful pattern, what brilliant colours! I shall tell the emperor that I like the cloth very much."[2]

"Be not afraid when a man becomes rich, when the glory of his house increases. For when he dies he will carry nothing away; his glory will not go down after him. For though, while he lives, he counts himself blessed—and though you get praise when you do well for yourself—his soul will go to the generation of his fathers, who will never again see light. Man in his pomp yet without understanding is like the beasts that perish" (Psalm 49:16–20 ESV).

"The fool says in his heart, 'There is no God.' They are corrupt, and their ways are vile; there is no one who does good" (Psalm 53:1 NIV).

"It is safer to meet a bear robbed of her cubs than to confront a fool caught in foolishness" (Proverbs 17:12 NLT).

"When you make a vow to God, do not be late in paying it; for He takes no delight in fools. Pay what you vow! It is better that you should not vow than that you should vow and not pay" (Ecclesiastes 5:4–5 NASB).

"Control your temper, for anger labels you a fool" (Ecclesiastes 7:9 NLT).

"Wine is a mocker and beer a brawler; whoever is led astray by them is not wise" (Proverbs 20:1 NIV).

"Putting confidence in an unreliable person in times of trouble is like chewing with a broken tooth or walking on a lame foot" (Proverbs 25:19 NLT).

"Do not answer a fool according to his folly, or you will be like him yourself" (Proverbs 26:4 NIV).

"He who trusts in his own heart is a fool" (Proverbs 28:26 NKJV).

"Professing to be wise, they became fools, and exchanged the glory of the incorruptible God for an image in the form of corruptible man and of birds and four-footed animals and crawling creatures" (Romans 1:22–23 NASB).

"Do not fool yourselves. If you think you are wise in this world, you should become a fool so that you can become truly wise, because the wisdom of this world is foolishness with God. It is written in the Scriptures, 'He catches those who are wise in their own clever traps.' It is also written in the Scriptures, 'The Lord knows what wise people think. He knows their thoughts are just a puff of wind'" (1 Corinthians 3:18–20 NCV).

Chapter 15

FOOLISH VS. WISE

A fool sees not the same tree that a wise man sees.
—William Blake, *The Marriage of Heaven and Hell*

In the previous chapter, we read quite a few Bible passages about the fool. Let's also focus on the wise man. To be a wise man (or woman), one must have understanding, knowledge, and discernment (what is right and true knowledge) with God's help. If God is not part of this, there will be no wisdom. Knowing that God is key to the process, we need to get into the habit of continually asking God to help us in our research, readings, and thought processes, so that we will make wise decisions, choices, and comments.

We may think that we are wise, but in God's eyes, we may only be the fool. Reading and meditating on God's Word will give us the discernment that is needed to be wise.

"Doing wickedness is like sport to a fool, and so is wisdom to a man of understanding" (Proverbs 10:23 NASB).

"The way of a fool is right in his own eyes, but he who heeds counsel is wise" (Proverbs 12:15 NKJV).

"Fools will believe anything, but the wise think about what they do. Someone with a quick temper does foolish things, but someone with understanding remains calm" (Proverbs 14:15, 17 NCV).

"The simple inherit folly, but the prudent are crowned with knowledge" (Proverbs 14:18 NIV).

"A ruler with no understanding will oppress his people, but one who hates corruption will have a long life" (Proverbs 28:16 NLT).

"A fool vents all his feelings, but a wise man holds them back" (Proverbs 29:11 NKJV).

Chapter 16

FORGIVENESS

To forgive can sometimes be easy and other times almost impossible. Now don't confuse forgiving with forgetting. We may not be able to forget, but we must forgive. God says we must forgive. God says if we do not forgive, He cannot forgive us. For me, those are two good reasons to forgive.

It also occurs to me that the individual who hurt me is a child of God too. He was given free will and made a poor or unthinkable choice. Why this person did this act is between God and him. My role is to forgive. If I don't, then I am creating a "dis-ease" in my body that can manifest into a disease.

To help you forgive, find a Bible passage that pertains to forgiveness and keep it close to your heart, so you can overcome your unforgiving spirit and be free. Dr. Charles Stanley of In Touch Ministries has a CD titled "Anger and Forgiveness" that you may find helpful.

"For if you forgive men when they sin against you, your heavenly Father will also forgive you. But if you do not forgive men their sins, your Father will not forgive your sins" (Matthew 6:14–15 NIV).

"'But that you may know that the Son of Man has power on earth to forgive sins'—then He said to the paralytic, 'Arise, take up your bed, and go to your house.' And he arose and departed to his house" (Matthew 9:6–7 NKJV).

"Then Peter came to Him and said, 'Lord, how often shall my brother sin against me, and I forgive him? Up to seven times?' Jesus said to him, 'I do not say to you, up to seven times, but up to seventy times seven'" (Matthew 18:21–22 NKJV).

"I acknowledged my sin to You, and my iniquity I did not hide; I said, 'I will confess my transgressions to the LORD'; and You forgave the guilt of my sin. Selah" (Psalm 32:5 NASB).

"And whenever you stand praying, if you have anything against anyone, forgive him, that your Father in heaven may also forgive you your trespasses. But if you do not forgive, neither will your Father in heaven forgive your trespasses" (Mark 11:25–26 NKJV).

"Forgive, and you will be forgiven" (Luke 6:37 ESV).

"So watch yourselves! If another believer sins, rebuke that person; then if there is repentance, forgive. Even if that person wrongs you seven times a day and each time turns again and asks forgiveness, you must forgive" (Luke 17:3–4 NLT).

"Get rid of all bitterness, rage, anger, harsh words, and slander, as well as all types of evil behavior. Instead, be kind to each other, tenderhearted, forgiving one another, just as God through Christ has forgiven you" (Ephesians 4:31–32 NLT).

"Put on then, as God's chosen ones, holy and beloved, compassionate hearts, kindness, humility, meekness, and patience, bearing with one another and, if one has a complaint against another, forgiving each other; as the Lord has forgiven you, so you also must forgive" (Colossians 3:12–13 ESV).

"If we confess our sins, He is faithful and righteous to forgive us our sins and to cleanse us from all unrighteousness" (1 John 1:9 NASB).

Chapter 17

GIVING AND CHARITY

You know the wonderful feeling of giving. It could have been a hug, a smile, a thank-you note, or the opportunity to see how your gift benefited others. You gave because you wanted to. It was an act of love, which will be blessed.

The word *charity* in the Bible means love for your fellowman. Your fellowman is everyone—strangers, friends, co-workers, the poor. There are thousands of charitable organizations that are helping people in need, but whom do you give to?

Since it is impossible to give to all charities, select the service that fits best with your beliefs. I thought I had found that charity until I discovered that my money was not accounted for through an audit of this organization. I now ask the organization for a financial statement before I donate money.

"Give generously to him and do so without a grudging heart; then because of this the LORD your God will bless you in all your work and in everything you put your hand to. There will always be poor people in the land. Therefore I command you to be openhanded toward your brothers and toward the poor and needy in your land" (Deuteronomy 15:10–11 NIV).

"A generous man will himself be blessed, for he shares his food with the poor" (Proverbs 22:9 NIV).

"If your enemy is hungry, give him bread to eat; and if he is thirsty, give him water to drink. . . . And the LORD will reward you" (Proverbs 25:21–22 NKJV).

"Whoever gives to the poor will not want, but he who hides his eyes will get many a curse" (Proverbs 28:27 ESV).

"Take heed that you do not do your charitable deeds before men, to be seen by them. Otherwise you have no reward from your Father in heaven. But . . . your charitable deed may be in secret; and your Father who sees in secret will Himself reward you openly" (Matthew 6:1, 3–4 NKJV).

"You should remember the words of the Lord Jesus: 'It is more blessed to give than to receive'" (Acts 20:35 NLT).

"Each one must give as he has decided in his heart, not reluctantly or under compulsion, for God loves a cheerful giver" (2 Corinthians 9:7 ESV).

Chapter 18

GOD'S INSTRUCTIONS— COMMANDMENTS

Just think, if we did not have any laws to obey, our society would be in anarchy. We are blessed to have a loving Father who had the wisdom to know that we needed guidance through statutes, laws, and precepts, which are the same as commandments.

Stop a moment and think. If everyone around the world followed the Ten Commandments (Exodus 20:1–17), can you imagine what our world would look like? The way we live, think, and communicate with each other would be entirely different. No more road rage, murders, security systems, lying, or breaking the laws. It would be like the idyllic town that we've read about in many fictional books. So until we find the idyllic town, we can follow God's instructions that will help us be better people and give us better lives.

"You shall not steal, nor deal falsely, nor lie to one another. And you shall not swear by My name falsely, nor shall you profane the name of your God: I am the LORD. You shall not cheat your neighbor, nor rob him. . . . You shall not curse the deaf, nor put a stumbling block before the blind, but shall fear your God: I am the LORD. You shall do no injustice in judgment. You shall not be partial to the poor, nor honor the person

53

of the mighty. In righteousness you shall judge your neighbor. You shall not go about as a talebearer among your people; nor shall you take a stand against the life of your neighbor: I am the LORD. You shall not hate your brother in your heart. You shall surely rebuke your neighbor, and not bear sin because of him. You shall not take vengeance, nor bear any grudge against the children of your people, but you shall love your neighbor as yourself: I am the LORD" (Leviticus 19:11–18 NKJV). Note: The word *talebearer* refers to one who spreads malicious stories or gossips, and the word *stand* means "to falsely accuse."

"So you shall keep My commandments, and do them; I am the LORD. 'You shall not profane My holy name'" (Leviticus 22:31–32 NASB).

"Thus you are to know in your heart that the LORD your God was disciplining you just as a man disciplines his son. Therefore, you shall keep the commandments of the LORD your God, to walk in His ways and to fear Him" (Deuteronomy 8:5–6 NASB).

"How can a young man cleanse his way? By taking heed according to Your word. With my whole heart I have sought You; Oh, let me not wander from Your commandments!" (Psalm 119:9–10 NKJV).

"He who keeps the commandment keeps his soul, but he who is careless of his ways will die" (Proverbs 19:16 NKJV).

"Only be very careful to observe the commandment and the law which Moses the servant of the LORD commanded you, to love the LORD your God and walk in all His ways and keep His commandments and hold fast to Him and serve Him with all your heart and with all your soul" (Joshua 22:5 NASB).

"Thus God has said, 'Why do you transgress the commandments of the LORD and do not prosper? Because you have forsaken the LORD, He has also forsaken you'" (2 Chronicles 24:20 NASB).

"If only you had paid attention to My commandments! Then your well-being would have been like a river, and your righteousness like the waves of the sea" (Isaiah 48:18 NASB).

"I am the LORD your God: Walk in My statutes, keep My judgments, and do them; hallow My Sabbaths, and they will be a sign between Me and you, that you may know that I am the LORD your God" (Ezekiel 20:19–20 NKJV).

"So in everything, do to others what you would have them do to you, for this sums up the Law and the Prophets" (Matthew 7:12 NIV).

"Jesus said to him, 'You shall love the LORD your God with all your heart, with all your soul, and with all your mind.' This is the first and great commandment. And the second is like it: 'You shall love your neighbor as yourself.' On these two commandments hang all the Law and the Prophets" (Matthew 22:37–40 NKJV).

"Jesus answered, 'The foremost is, "Hear, O Israel! The LORD our God is one LORD; and you shall love the LORD your God with all your heart, and with all your soul, and with all your mind, and with all your strength." The second is this, "You shall love your neighbor as yourself." There is no other commandment greater than these'" (Mark 12:29–31 NASB).

"And Jesus answered him, 'It is written, "Man shall not live by bread alone"'" (Luke 4:4 ESV).

"But I tell you who hear me: Love your enemies, do good to those who hate you, bless those who curse you, pray for those who mistreat you" (Luke 6:27–28 NIV).

"I will meditate on Your precepts, and contemplate Your ways. I will delight myself in Your statutes; I will not forget Your word" (Psalm 119:15–16 NKJV).

"This is My commandment, that you love one another as I have loved you. Greater love has no one than this, than to lay down one's life for his friends" (John 15:12–13 NKJV).

"What matters is the keeping of the commandments of God" (1 Corinthians 7:19 NASB).

"It is good for me that I was afflicted, that I may learn Your statutes. The law of Your mouth is better to me than thousands of gold and silver pieces. Your hands made me and fashioned me; give me understanding, that I may learn Your commandments" (Psalm 119:71–73 NASB).

"I gain understanding from your precepts; therefore I hate every wrong path" (Psalm 119:104 NIV).

"Hold me up, and I shall be safe, and I shall observe Your statutes continually. You reject all those who stray from Your statutes, for their deceit is falsehood" (Psalm 119:117–118 NKJV).

"Trouble and anguish have come upon me, yet Your commandments are my delight" (Psalm 119:143 NASB).

"Many are my persecutors and my adversaries, yet I do not turn aside from Your testimonies. I behold the treacherous and loathe them, because they do not keep Your word" (Psalm 119:157–158 NASB).

"I rejoice at Your word, as one who finds great spoil. I hate and despise falsehood, but I love Your law" (Psalm 119:162–163 NASB).

"Let Your hand be ready to help me, for I have chosen Your precepts" (Psalm 119:173 NASB).

"Whoever despises the word brings destruction on himself, but he who reveres the commandment will be rewarded" (Proverbs 13:13 ESV).

"Now the purpose of the commandment is love from a pure heart, from a good conscience, and from sincere faith, from which some, having strayed, have turned aside to idle talk, desiring to be teachers of the law, understanding neither what they say nor the things which they affirm" (1 Timothy 1:5–7 NKJV).

"By this we know that we have come to know Him, if we keep His commandments" (1 John 2:3 NASB).

"This is His commandment, that we believe in the name of His Son Jesus Christ, and love one another, just as He commanded us" (1 John 3:23 NASB).

"If someone says, 'I love God,' and hates his brother, he is a liar; for he who does not love his brother whom he has seen, how can he love God whom he has not seen? And this commandment we have from Him: that he who loves God must love his brother also" (1 John 4:20–21 NKJV).

"For this is the love of God, that we keep His commandments; and His commandments are not burdensome" (1 John 5:3 NASB).

"This is love, that we walk according to His commandments. This is the commandment, that as you have heard from the beginning, you should walk in it" (2 John 1:6 NKJV).

Chapter 19

GOODNESS

There is a struggle between good and evil, which all began in the garden of Eden with the tree of the knowledge of good and evil. If we have a choice of being good or evil, we inherently know that we want to be good. God, who created us, is *omnibenevolence*—perfect goodness. In order to be good, since we are all sinners, we need to be open to correction. So be wise in your choices, because there will always be consequences to your choices.

> "Goodness does not consist in greatness, but greatness in goodness."
>
> —Athenaeus

"For the LORD is good . . ." (Psalm 100:5 NIV).

"If you plan to do evil, you will be lost; if you plan to do good, you will receive unfailing love and faithfulness" (Proverbs 14:22 NLT).

"What is desirable in a man is his kindness" (Proverbs 19:22 NASB).

"I know that there is nothing better for men than to be happy and do good while they live. That everyone may eat and drink, and find satisfaction in all his toil—this is the gift of God" (Ecclesiastes 3:12–13 NIV).

"If a man fathers a hundred children and lives many years, so that the days of his years are many, but his soul is not satisfied with life's good things, and he also has no burial, I say that a stillborn child is better off than he" (Ecclesiastes 6:3 ESV).

"Put away the evil of your doings from before My eyes. Cease to do evil, learn to do good; seek justice, rebuke the oppressor; defend the fatherless, plead for the widow" (Isaiah 1:16–17 NKJV).

"This is what the LORD says: As I have brought all this great calamity on this people, so I will give them all the prosperity I have promised them" (Jeremiah 32:42 NIV).

"The LORD is good to those who wait for Him, to the person who seeks Him. It is good that he waits silently for the salvation of the LORD" (Lamentations 3:25–26 NASB).

"Cling to what is good" (Romans 12:9 NKJV).

"Do not be overcome by evil, but overcome evil with good" (Romans 12:21 ESV).

"We should help others do what is right and build them up in the Lord" (Romans 15:2 NLT).

"Therefore, as we have opportunity, let us do good to all people, especially to those who belong to the family of believers" (Galatians 6:10 NIV).

"See that no one repays anyone evil for evil, but always seek to do good to one another and to everyone" (1 Thessalonians 5:15 ESV).

"But examine everything carefully; hold fast to that which is good" (1 Thessalonians 5:21 NASB).

"Since everything God created is good, we should not reject any of it but receive it with thanks" (1 Timothy 4:4 NLT).

"All Scripture is inspired by God and profitable for teaching, for reproof, for correction, for training in righteousness; so that the man of God may be adequate, equipped for every good work" (2 Timothy 3:16–17 NASB).

"This is a faithful saying, and these things I will that thou affirm constantly, that they which have believed in God might be careful to maintain good works. These things are good and profitable unto men" (Titus 3:8 KJV).

"For it is God's will that by doing good you should silence the ignorant talk of foolish men" (1 Peter 2:15 NIV).

"Beloved, do not imitate what is evil, but what is good. The one who does good is of God; the one who does evil has not seen God" (3 John 1:11 NASB).

Chapter 20

GRACE

Amazing grace, how sweet the sound,
That saved a wretch like me.
I once was lost but now am found,
Was blind, but now I see.
—John Newton, "Amazing Grace"

My mother's apartment was across from the cemetery. Frequently, when I was home to visit her, there would be a funeral. I will never forget hearing the bagpipes play the beloved song "Amazing Grace" as the people were gathering at the gravesite. My heart literally leaped! You may have had that experience too.

Grace is God's unmerited favor to us. Every day, we enjoy God's good gifts when we don't deserve them. Blessed are we.

"But by the grace of God I am what I am, and His grace toward me was not in vain; but I labored more abundantly than they all, yet not I, but the grace of God which was with me" (1 Corinthians 15:10 NKJV).

"Now this is our boast: . . . not according to worldly wisdom but according to God's grace" (2 Corinthians 1:12 NIV).

"And He said to me, 'My grace is sufficient for you, for My strength is made perfect in weakness'" (2 Corinthians 12:9 NKJV).

"I do not nullify the grace of God, for if righteousness were through the law, then Christ died for no purpose" (Galatians 2:21 ESV).

"In Him we have redemption through His blood, the forgiveness of sins, according to the riches of His grace which He made to abound toward us in all wisdom and prudence" (Ephesians 1:7–8 NKJV).

"But God, who is rich in mercy, because of His great love with which He loved us, even when we were dead in trespasses, made us alive together with Christ (by grace you have been saved)" (Ephesians 2:4–5 NKJV).

"May God's grace be eternally upon all who love our Lord Jesus Christ" (Ephesians 6:24 NLT).

Chapter 21

HAPPINESS AND JOY

I'm sure you can recall joyful moments in your life. Maybe it was the first time holding your baby or a promotion or graduation or being surrounded by family and friends. God orchestrates and produces these joyful moments to fill us up with gratitude.

"Joyful, Joyful, We Adore Thee" is probably a familiar song to you. Sometimes it is nice just to read the words. Here are the first and last verses of the song.

Joyful, joyful, we adore Thee, God of glory, Lord of love;
Hearts unfold like flowers before Thee,
      opening to the sun above.
Melt the clouds of sin and sadness;
      drive the dark of doubt away;
Giver of immortal gladness, fill us with the light of day!

Mortals, join the happy chorus,
      which the morning stars began;
Father love is reigning o'er us,
      brother love binds man to man.
Ever singing, march we onward,
      victors in the midst of strife,
Joyful music leads us Sunward in the triumph song of life.
                                                  —Henry J. van Dyke

"But let all those rejoice who put their trust in You; let them ever shout for joy, because You defend them; let those also who love Your name be joyful in You" (Psalm 5:11 NKJV).

"And my soul shall be joyful in the LORD; it shall rejoice in His salvation" (Psalm 35:9 NKJV).

"Unto God my exceeding joy" (Psalm 43:4 KJV).

"Make a joyful noise to the LORD, all the earth; break forth into joyous song and sing praises!" (Psalm 98:4 ESV).

"Happy is the man who finds wisdom, and the man who gains understanding; for her proceeds are better than the profits of silver, and her gain than fine gold. She is more precious than rubies, and all the things you may desire cannot compare with her" (Proverbs 3:13–15 NKJV).

"Moreover, when God gives any man wealth and possessions, and enables him to enjoy them, to accept his lot and be happy in his work—this is a gift of God. He seldom reflects on the days of his life, because God keeps him occupied with gladness of heart" (Ecclesiastes 5:19–20 NIV).

"It was fitting to celebrate and be glad, for this your brother was dead, and is alive; he was lost, and is found" (Luke 15:32 ESV).

"He who heeds the word wisely will find good, and whoever trusts in the LORD, happy is he" (Proverbs 16:20 NKJV).

"Happy is the man who is always reverent, but he who hardens his heart will fall into calamity" (Proverbs 28:14 NKJV).

"For You, LORD, have made me glad through Your work; I will triumph in the works of Your hands" (Psalm 92:4 NKJV).

"Make a joyful shout to the Lord, all you lands! Serve the Lord with gladness; come before His presence with singing" (Psalm 100:1–2 NKJV).

"This is the day the Lord has made. We will rejoice and be glad in it" (Psalm 118:24 NLT).

"You will enjoy the fruit of your labor. How joyful and prosperous you will be!" (Psalm 128:2 NLT).

Chapter 22

HEALTH

Or do you not know that your body is the temple of the
Holy Spirit who is in you, whom you have from God,
and you are not your own?
—1 Corinthians 6:19 NKJV

God created our bodies and gave them life, perfect without disease
or pain; but because of disobedience, we are susceptible to ill
health. Take heed what you put into your mouth. Two well-known
facts are not to overeat or smoke. Of course, there are many others, but
I am not writing a book on nutrition. If you are interested, there is a
section in the Old Testament, Leviticus 11, that states what foods you
should and should not eat.

Also be careful what you are feeding your mind for your emotional
health. Are your thoughts uplifting or negative? Negative thoughts
arising from an anxiety-driven, stressful life can cause a number of
ailments, including high blood pressure, back pain, extreme tiredness,
and headaches.

Here is something to keep in mind: Negative thoughts create negative
emotions, which create a weakened immune system. Positive thoughts
create positive emotions, which create a strong immune system.

"Do not be wise in your own eyes; fear the LORD and depart from evil. It will be health to your flesh, and strength to your bones" (Proverbs 3:7–8 NKJV).

"Reckless words pierce like a sword, but the tongue of the wise brings healing" (Proverbs 12:18 NIV).

"A sound heart is life to the body, but envy is rottenness to the bones" (Proverbs 14:30 NKJV).

"A cheerful look brings joy to the heart; good news makes for good health" (Proverbs 15:30 NLT).

"Pleasant words are like a honeycomb, sweetness to the soul and health to the bones" (Proverbs 16:24 NKJV).

"A joyful heart is good medicine, but a broken spirit dries up the bones" (Proverbs 17:22 NASB).

"No longer drink only water, but use a little wine for the sake of your stomach and your frequent ailments" (1 Timothy 5:23 ESV).

Chapter 23

HEART

The heart (representing our inner person) breaks, aches, loves, fills with joy, bursts with pride, yearns, deceives, grieves, and hates. Our physical heart has the function of keeping us alive and supplying all of our cells with oxygen. The heart reveals the man.

When you have had a decision to make, your friend may have said, "Listen to your heart." No doubt you have heard this phrase: "Let's have a heart-to-heart talk." That's that serious, intimate talk. The heart is the center from which all projects outward.

Because our hearts are so important, it is imperative that we guard our hearts, purify our hearts, and let God rule our hearts.

"God is my shield, saving those whose hearts are true and right" (Psalm 7:10 NLT).

"Those who are of a perverse heart are an abomination to the LORD, but the blameless in their ways are His delight" (Proverbs 11:20 NKJV).

"All the days of the oppressed are wretched, but the cheerful heart has a continual feast" (Proverbs 15:15 NIV).

"But the LORD said to Samuel, 'Do not look at his appearance or at his physical stature, because I have refused him. For the LORD does not see as man sees; for man looks at the outward appearance, but the LORD looks at the heart'" (1 Samuel 16:7 NKJV).

"Many are the plans in a man's heart, but it is the LORD's purpose that prevails" (Proverbs 19:21 NIV).

"Every way of a man is right in his own eyes, but the LORD weighs the heart" (Proverbs 21:2 ESV).

"The LORD is God; there is no other. Let your heart therefore be loyal to the LORD our God, to walk in His statutes and keep His commandments, as at this day" (1 Kings 8:60–61 NKJV).

"Since I know, O my God, that You try the heart and delight in uprightness" (1 Chronicles 29:17 NASB).

"And he said: 'LORD God of Israel, there is no God in heaven or on earth like You, who keep Your covenant and mercy with Your servants who walk before You with all their hearts'" (2 Chronicles 6:14 NKJV). Note: This was spoken by King Solomon.

"As in water face reflects face, so a man's heart reveals the man" (Proverbs 27:19 NKJV).

"O continue Your lovingkindness to those who know You, and Your righteousness to the upright in heart" (Psalm 36:10 NASB).

"Extortion turns a wise man into a fool, and a bribe corrupts the heart" (Ecclesiastes 7:7 NIV).

"Harlotry, wine, and new wine enslave the heart" (Hosea 4:11 NKJV).

"Do not let your heart be troubled; believe in God, believe also in Me" (John 14:1 NASB). Note: *Me* refers to Jesus.

"Delight yourself also in the LORD, and He shall give you the desires of your heart" (Psalm 37:4 NKJV).

"Do not let your adorning be external—the braiding of hair and the putting on of gold jewelry, or the clothing you wear—but let your adorning be the hidden person of the heart with the imperishable beauty of a gentle and quiet spirit, which in God's sight is very precious" (1 Peter 3:3–4 ESV).

"If riches increase, set not your heart upon them" (Psalm 62:10 KJV).

"Do not let my heart incline to any evil, to busy myself with wicked deeds in company with men who work iniquity, and let me not eat of their delicacies!" (Psalm 141:4 ESV).

Chapter 24

HELL

Hell is the highest reward that the devil can offer
you for being a servant of his.
—Billy Sunday, American evangelist, 1862–1935

All aboard! All aboard the hell train!

It is your choice. How will you spend your eternal life—in heaven or hell?

The Bible refers to living in hell as "cast down," "down to death," "die in your sins," "deserving of death," "the way of death," and "dead."

Some people believe that there is no such place as hell, or that it is only in the mind, or that it is here on earth. Believe it or not, God says there is a hell (Luke 12:5). You can only have eternal life with God by believing in Jesus (John 3:15). If not, you will be boarding the hell train and watching the paradise train going off on a different track.

Know Jesus. Believe in Him. He is the way away from hell.

"From those who leave the paths of uprightness to walk in the ways of darkness; who rejoice in doing evil, and delight in the perversity of the wicked; whose ways are crooked, and who are devious in their paths; to deliver you from the immoral woman, from the seductress who flatters with her words, who forsakes the companion of her youth, and forgets the covenant of her God. For her house leads down to death, and her paths to the dead" (Proverbs 2:13–18 NKJV).

"Because you have said, 'We have made a covenant with death, . . . for we have made lies our refuge, and in falsehood we have taken shelter'" (Isaiah 28:15 ESV).

"'Were they ashamed because of the abomination they have done? They were not even ashamed at all; they did not even know how to blush. Therefore they shall fall among those who fall; at the time that I punish them, they shall be cast down,' says the LORD" (Jeremiah 6:15 NASB).

"Let death seize them; let them go down alive into hell, for wickedness is in their dwellings and among them" (Psalm 55:15 NKJV).

"And He said to them, 'You are from beneath; I am from above. You are of this world; I am not of this world. Therefore I said to you that you will die in your sins; for if you do not believe that I am He, you will die in your sins'" (John 8:23–24 NKJV).

"And even as they did not like to retain God in their knowledge, God gave them over to a debased mind, to do those things which are not fitting; being filled with all unrighteousness, sexual immorality, wickedness, covetousness, maliciousness; full of envy, murder, strife, deceit, evil-mindedness; they are whisperers, backbiters, haters of God, violent, proud, boasters, inventors of evil things, disobedient to parents, undiscerning, untrustworthy, unloving, unforgiving, unmerciful; who, knowing the righteous judgment of God, that those who practice such things are deserving of death, not only do the same but also approve of those who practice them" (Romans 1:28–32 NKJV).

"For if you live according to the flesh you will die" (Romans 8:13 ESV).

"You who are trying to be justified by law have been alienated from Christ; you have fallen away from grace" (Galatians 5:4 NIV).

"There is a way which seems right to a man, but its end is the way of death" (Proverbs 14:12 NASB).

"The coming of the lawless one is according to the working of Satan, with all power, signs, and lying wonders, and with all unrighteous deception among those who perish, because they did not receive the love of the truth, that they might be saved. And for this reason God will send them strong delusion, that they should believe the lie, that they all may be condemned who did not believe the truth but had pleasure in unrighteousness" (2 Thessalonians 2:9–12 NKJV).

"And to whom did He swear that they would not enter His rest, but to those who did not obey? So we see that they could not enter in because of unbelief" (Hebrews 3:18–19 NKJV).

Chapter 25

HOLY SPIRIT

Christians believe in the Trinity. The Trinity is the Father (God), the Son (Jesus), and the Holy Spirit. One God exists in three persons. "So there are three witnesses in heaven: the Father, the Word and the Holy Spirit and these three are One" (1 John 5:7 AMP). The *Word* is Jesus.

Below is a simple illustration of the Trinity that will help you understand the Holy Spirit in the Bible passages.

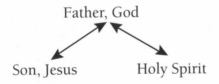

They are all God.

The Holy Spirit dwells in believers. He is the power source who intercedes for us, reveals truth, and guides us during our daily activities. "For prophecy never came by the will of man, but holy men of God spoke as they were moved by the Holy Spirit" (2 Peter 1:21 NKJV).

"But when the Helper comes, whom I shall send to you from the Father, the Spirit of truth who proceeds from the Father, He will testify of Me" (John 15:26 NKJV). Note: The *Helper* is the Holy Spirit.

"And God, who knows the heart, testified to them giving them the Holy Spirit, just as He also did to us; and He made no distinction between us and them, cleansing their hearts by faith" (Acts 15:8–9 NASB). Note: Peter is talking here about Gentiles (non-Jewish) people.

"No one knows the thoughts of God except the Spirit of God. We have not received the spirit of the world but the Spirit who is from God, that we may understand what God has freely given us" (1 Corinthians 2:11–12 NIV).

"Do you not know that you are God's temple and that God's Spirit dwells in you?" (1 Corinthians 3:16 ESV).

"Or do you not know that your body is the temple of the Holy Spirit who is in you, whom you have from God, and you are not your own? For you were bought at a price; therefore glorify God in your body and in your spirit, which are God's" (1 Corinthians 6:19–20 NKJV).

"For the Lord is the Spirit, and wherever the Spirit of the Lord is, there is freedom" (2 Corinthians 3:17 NLT).

"For we through the Spirit, by faith, are waiting for the hope of righteousness" (Galatians 5:5 NASB).

"I say then: Walk in the Spirit, and you shall not fulfill the lust of the flesh. For the flesh lusts against the Spirit, and the Spirit against the flesh; and these are contrary to one another, so that you do not do the things that you wish" (Galatians 5:16–17 NKJV).

"But the fruit of the Spirit is love, joy, peace, patience, kindness, goodness, faithfulness, gentleness, self-control; against such things there is no law. And those who belong to Christ Jesus have crucified the flesh with its passions and desires. If we live by the Spirit, let us also walk by the Spirit. Let us not become conceited, provoking one another, envying one another" (Galatians 5:22–26 ESV).

"For this reason I bow my knees to the Father of our Lord Jesus Christ, from whom the whole family in heaven and earth is named, that He would grant you, according to the riches of His glory, to be strengthened with might through His Spirit in the inner man, that Christ may dwell in your hearts through faith; that you, being rooted and grounded in love, may be able to comprehend with all the saints what is the width and length and depth and height—to know the love of Christ which passes knowledge; that you may be filled with all the fullness of God" (Ephesians 3:14–19 NKJV).

"Do not quench (suppress or subdue) the [Holy] Spirit" (1 Thessalonians 5:19 AMP).

Chapter 26

HOPE

Consult not your fears but your hopes and dreams. Think not about your frustrations, but about your unfulfilled potential. Concern yourself not with what you tried and failed in, but with what is still possible for you to do.
—Pope John XXIII

Hope is the companion of power, and mother of success; for who so hopes strongly has within him the gift of miracles.
—Samuel Smiles

Life would be more difficult if we didn't have hope. This four-letter word gives you a zest to keep going through the worst of times. Hope affects your attitude and your way of thinking. Hope is stimulating.

Nothing is ever hopeless, except in your own mind. You create hopeless scenarios by focusing on negative outcomes. Replace your thoughts with positive outcomes so they will elevate you. Never lose hope!

"'The LORD is my portion,' says my soul, 'therefore I have hope in Him'" (Lamentations 3:24 NASB).

"Be of good courage, and He shall strengthen your heart, all you who hope in the LORD" (Psalm 31:24 NKJV).

"Why are you in despair, O my soul? And why have you become disturbed within me? Hope in God, for I shall again praise Him for the help of His presence" (Psalm 42:5 NASB).

"Why are you cast down, O my soul? And why are you disquieted within me? Hope in God; for I shall yet praise Him, the help of my countenance and my God" (Psalm 42:11 NKJV). Note: You will find this same passage in Psalm 43:5.

"We will not hide them from their children, telling to the generation to come the praises of the LORD, and His strength and His wonderful works that He has done. For He established a testimony in Jacob, and appointed a law in Israel, which He commanded our fathers, that they should make them known to their children; that the generation to come might know them, the children who would be born, that they may arise and declare them to their children, that they may set their hope in God, and not forget the works of God, but keep His commandments" (Psalm 78:4–7 NKJV).

"Hope deferred makes the heart sick, but a longing fulfilled is a tree of life" (Proverbs 13:12 NIV).

"Not only so, but we also rejoice in our sufferings, because we know that suffering produces perseverance; perseverance, character; and character, hope" (Romans 5:3–4 NIV).

"Now hope does not disappoint, because the love of God has been poured out in our hearts by the Holy Spirit who was given to us" (Romans 5:5 NKJV).

"For whatever was written in former days was written for our instruction, that through endurance and through the encouragement of the Scriptures we might have hope" (Romans 15:4 ESV).

"Now may the God of hope fill you with all joy and peace in believing, that you may abound in hope by the power of the Holy Spirit" (Romans 15:13 NKJV).

"You are my hiding place and my shield; I hope in Your word" (Psalm 119:114 NKJV).

"But Christ, as the Son, is in charge of God's entire house. And we are God's house, if we keep our courage and remain confident in our hope in Christ" (Hebrews 3:6 NLT).

"This hope we have as an anchor of the soul, both sure and steadfast" (Hebrews 6:19 NKJV).

"Know that wisdom is thus for your soul; if you find it, then there will be a future, and your hope will not be cut off" (Proverbs 24:14 NASB).

Chapter 27

HUMILITY

You might remember when Mac Davis made this a popular song, "It's Hard To Be Humble." One line from the refrain says, "Oh Lord it's hard to be humble when you're perfect in every way."

This always makes me laugh and smile. How can anyone be so in love with himself? Well, I am sure that there were times that I thought I was "Miss Wonderful," only to have the pedestal knocked out from under me. To stay humble, always be teachable and accept correction. Another thought that will humble us quickly is that God will always be better than we are. So when we feel pride swelling up in us, we must focus on God.

"Can a mortal be more righteous than God? Can a man be more pure than his Maker?" (Job 4:17 NIV).

"Let another man praise you, and not your own mouth; a stranger, and not your own lips" (Proverbs 27:2 NKJV).

"So anyone who becomes as humble as this little child is the greatest in the Kingdom of Heaven" (Matthew 18:4 NLT).

"For everyone who exalts himself will be humbled, and he who humbles himself will be exalted" (Luke 14:11 NIV).

"Live in harmony with each other. Don't be too proud to enjoy the company of ordinary people. And don't think you know it all!" (Romans 12:16 NLT).

"The LORD lifts up the humble; he casts the wicked to the ground" (Psalm 147:6 ESV).

"For the LORD takes delight in his people; he crowns the humble with salvation" (Psalm 149:4 NIV).

"But we have this treasure in earthen vessels, so that the surpassing greatness of the power will be of God and not from ourselves" (2 Corinthians 4:7 NASB).

"Surely He scorns the scornful, but gives grace to the humble" (Proverbs 3:34 NKJV).

"The reward for humility and fear of the LORD is riches and honor and life" (Proverbs 22:4 ESV).

"But the brother of humble circumstances is to glory in his high position; and the rich man is to glory in his humiliation, because like flowering grass he will pass away" (James 1:9–10 NASB).

"Humble yourselves in the sight of the Lord, and He will lift you up" (James 4:10 NKJV).

"Therefore humble yourselves under the mighty hand of God, that He may exalt you in due time, casting all your care upon Him, for He cares for you" (1 Peter 5:6–7 NKJV).

Chapter 28

IMPARTIALITY

The picture of Lady Justice shows her holding an even scale with a blindfold across her eyes, depicting her impartiality when making a judgment. God shows no partiality. He doesn't care where we fit in men's eyes, because our sin will be punished and our righteousness will be blessed on its own merit.

You may have heard this wonderful story. Several businessmen were in a meeting late, and they had to rush to catch their flight if they were going to be home in time for dinner. As they ran through the airport to catch their flight, they stumbled over a table with apples on it. A blind woman was selling the apples. The apples scattered all over the floor. They looked back but kept running, because they couldn't miss their flight.

One of the businessmen couldn't get the incident out of his mind, so he told his friend to call his wife and let her know he would be late getting home. He went back to the blind woman, who was on her hands and knees trying to find her apples. This man picked the apples up and replaced them on the table.

As he walked away, the woman said to him, "Mister, are you Jesus?"

Wouldn't it be wonderful if we could just see each person as God does? We are all His children and equal in His eyes. Poor, rich, gifted or not, we will be treated the same. Do you treat everyone the same?

When you see people who don't quite fit into your thinking about what's acceptable, do you treat them the same as you would a friend?

"You shall not show partiality to a poor man in his dispute" (Exodus 23:3 NKJV).

"You shall not pervert justice. You shall not show partiality, and you shall not accept a bribe, for a bribe blinds the eyes of the wise and subverts the cause of the righteous" (Deuteronomy 16:19 ESV).

"Who shows no partiality to princes nor regards the rich above the poor, for they all are the work of His hands?" (Job 34:19 NASB).

"As for the Almighty, we cannot find Him; He is excellent in power, in judgment and abundant justice; He does not oppress. Therefore men fear Him; He shows no partiality to any who are wise of heart" (Job 37:23–24 NKJV).

"He will bless those who fear the LORD, both small and great" (Psalm 115:13 NKJV).

"Slaves, be obedient to those who are your masters according to the flesh, with fear and trembling, in the sincerity of your heart, as to Christ; not by way of eyeservice, as men-pleasers, but as slaves of Christ, doing the will of God from the heart. With good will render service, as to the Lord, and not to men, knowing that whatever good thing each one does, this he will receive back from the Lord, whether slave or free. And masters, do the same things to them, and give up threatening, knowing that both their Master and yours is in heaven, and there is no partiality with Him" (Ephesians 6:5–9 NASB).

"Anyone who does wrong will be repaid for his wrong, and there is no favoritism" (Colossians 3:25 NIV).

"These also are sayings of the wise. Partiality in judging is not good. Whoever says to the wicked, 'You are in the right,' will be cursed by peoples, abhorred by nations, but those who rebuke the wicked will have delight, and a good blessing will come upon them" (Proverbs 24:23–25 ESV).

"Showing partiality is never good, yet some will do wrong for a mere piece of bread" (Proverbs 28:21 NLT).

"The poor man and the oppressor have this in common: The LORD gives light to the eyes of both" (Proverbs 29:13 NKJV).

Chapter 29

ISRAEL

Israel is the very embodiment of Jewish continuity: It is the only nation on earth that inhabits the same land, bears the same name, speaks the same language, and worships the same God that it did 3,000 years ago. You dig the soil and you find pottery from Davidic times, coins from Bar Kokhba, and 2,000-year-old scrolls written in a script remarkably like the one that today advertises ice cream at the corner candy store.
—Charles Krauthammer

God promised the land of Israel to Abraham, Isaac, and Jacob. This is the land of the Jews, God's chosen people. The International Fellowship of Christians and Jews is one organization that is carrying out God's Word by helping the Jewish communities throughout the world. Remember, "I will bless those who bless you" (Genesis 12:3 NKJV). Be a blessing to God by helping and praying for the Jews.

"Now the LORD said to Abram, 'Go from your country and your kindred and your father's house to the land that I will show you. And I will make of you a great nation, and I will bless you and make your name great, so that you will be a blessing. I will bless those who bless you, and him who dishonors you I will curse, and in you all the families of the earth shall be blessed'" (Genesis 12:1–3 ESV). Note: God is speaking here to Abram, whom He later renamed Abraham.

"For You have made Your people Israel Your very own people forever; and You, LORD, have become their God" (1 Chronicles 17:22 NKJV).

"Praise be to the LORD, the God of Israel, from everlasting to everlasting. Let all the people say, 'Amen!' Praise the LORD" (Psalm 106:48 NIV).

"Pray for peace in Jerusalem. May all who love this city prosper" (Psalm 122:6 NLT).

"O Israel, hope in the LORD; for with the LORD there is mercy, and with Him is abundant redemption. And He shall redeem Israel from all his iniquities" (Psalm 130:7–8 NKJV).

"Israel has been saved by the LORD with an everlasting salvation; you will not be put to shame or humiliated to all eternity" (Isaiah 45:17 NASB).

"Listen to Me, you stubborn-hearted, who are far from righteousness: I bring My righteousness near, it shall not be far off; My salvation shall not linger. And I will place salvation in Zion, for Israel My glory" (Isaiah 46:12–13 NKJV).

"O LORD, the hope of Israel, all who forsake You will be put to shame" (Jeremiah 17:13 NASB).

"They shall be My people, and I will be their God; then I will give them one heart and one way, that they may fear Me forever, for the good of them and their children after them. And I will make an everlasting covenant with them, that I will not turn away from doing them good; but I will put My fear in their hearts so that they will not depart from Me. Yes, I will rejoice over them to do them good, and I will assuredly plant them in this land, with all My heart and with all My soul" (Jeremiah 32:38–41 NKJV).

Chapter 30

JESUS

I have read in Plato and Cicero sayings that are very wise and very beautiful; but I never read in either of them: "Come unto me all ye that labour and are heavy laden."
—St. Augustine

Merry Christmas! December 25 is the day the world celebrates the birthday of Jesus—Prince of Peace, Savior, God incarnate (God in human form), Son of God, Shepherd, Teacher, Christ, and Overseer.

We do not know the exact birth date of Jesus, but that seems insignificant compared to His purpose on earth. Jesus came not to judge but to teach us how to live, to serve His fellowman, and to save us from our sins. Revisit Jesus by entering into His Word and letting it awaken your soul. You too can be reborn in Jesus.

"Behold, the virgin shall conceive and bear a Son, and shall call His name Immanuel" (Isaiah 7:14 NKJV). Note: *Immanuel* means "God with us."

"For a child will be born to us, a son will be given to us; and the government will rest on His shoulders; and His name will be called Wonderful Counselor, Mighty God, Eternal Father, Prince of Peace. There will be no end to the increase of His government or of peace" (Isaiah 9:6–7 NASB).

"And a great windstorm arose, and the waves beat into the boat, so that it was already filling. But He was in the stern, asleep on a pillow. And they awoke Him and said to Him, 'Teacher, do You not care that we are perishing?' Then He arose and rebuked the wind, and said to the sea, 'Peace, be still!' And the wind ceased and there was a great calm. But He said to them, 'Why are you so fearful? How is it that you have no faith?' And they feared exceedingly, and said to one another, 'Who can this be, that even the wind and the sea obey Him!'" (Mark 4:37–41 NKJV).

"Yet it shall not be so among you; but whoever desires to become great among you shall be your servant. And whoever of you desires to be first shall be slave of all. For even the Son of Man did not come to be served, but to serve, and to give His life a ransom for many" (Mark 10:43–45 NKJV).

"But as many as received Him, to them He gave the right to become children of God, to those who believe in His name: who were born, not of blood, nor of the will of the flesh, nor of the will of man, but of God. And the Word became flesh and dwelt among us, and we beheld His glory, the glory as of the only begotten of the Father, full of grace and truth" (John 1:12–14 NKJV). Note: *Word became flesh* is referring to Jesus.

"I can do nothing on My own initiative. As I hear, I judge; and My judgment is just, because I do not seek My own will, but the will of Him who sent Me" (John 5:30 NASB).

"I know Him, because I am from Him, and He sent Me" (John 7:29 NASB). Note: Jesus is speaking.

"Jesus said to them, 'If God were your Father, you would love Me, for I proceeded forth and came from God; nor have I come of Myself, but He sent Me'" (John 8:42 NKJV).

"Christ Jesus came into the world to save sinners" (1 Timothy 1:15 NLT).

"It is a trustworthy statement: for if we died with Him, we will also live with Him; if we endure, we will also reign with Him; if we deny Him, He also will deny us; if we are faithless, He remains faithful, for He cannot deny Himself" (2 Timothy 2:11–13 NASB).

"God . . . has in these last days spoken to us by His Son, whom He has appointed heir of all things" (Hebrews 1:1–2 NKJV).

"With His own blood He entered the Most Holy Place once for all, having obtained eternal redemption" (Hebrews 9:12 NKJV).

"Jesus Christ is the same yesterday and today and forever" (Hebrews 13:8 NIV).

"But when you do good and suffer, if you take it patiently, this is commendable before God. For to this you were called, because Christ also suffered for us, leaving us an example, that you should follow His steps: 'Who committed no sin, nor was deceit found in His mouth'; who, when He was reviled, did not revile in return; when He suffered, He did not threaten, but committed Himself to Him who judges righteously; who Himself bore our sins in His own body on the tree, that we, having died to sins, might live for righteousness—by whose stripes you were healed. For you were like sheep going astray, but have now returned to the Shepherd and Overseer of your souls" (1 Peter 2:20–25 NKJV).

"He is the atoning sacrifice for our sins, and not only for ours but also for the sins of the whole world" (1 John 2:2 NIV).

"And from Jesus Christ, the faithful witness, the firstborn from the dead, and the ruler over the kings of the earth. To Him who loved us and washed us from our sins in His own blood, and has made us kings and priests to His God and Father, to Him be glory and dominion forever and ever. Amen" (Revelation 1:5–6 NKJV).

Chapter 31

JESUS CRUCIFIED
AND RISEN

We begin with Maundy Thursday: the Last Supper; then go to Good Friday: Jesus dies on the cross, taking on all of our sins; then on to Easter: Jesus rises from the dead, not as a ghost but in human form. The reason for His death was to save us.

The magnitude of God's love for you and me is incomprehensible to me. Our God, who created each one of us, gave His only Son to die for you and me, because God knew that we could not be sinless. God had Jesus crucified so that we could have eternal life with Him. Now that is love.

> In that old rugged cross, stained with blood so divine,
> a wondrous beauty I see,
> for 'twas on that old cross Jesus suffered and died,
> to pardon and sanctify me.
> —George Bennard, "The Old Rugged Cross"

"And while they were gathering together in Galilee, Jesus said to them, 'The Son of Man is going to be delivered into the hands of men; and they will kill Him, and He will be raised on the third day'" (Matthew 17:22–23 NASB).

"Just as the Son of Man did not come to be served, but to serve, and to give His life a ransom for many" (Matthew 20:28 NKJV).

"He then began to teach them that the Son of Man must suffer many things and be rejected by the elders, chief priests and teachers of the law, and that he must be killed and after three days rise again" (Mark 8:31 NIV).

"For He taught His disciples and said to them, 'The Son of Man is being betrayed into the hands of men, and they will kill Him. And after He is killed, He will rise the third day'" (Mark 9:31 NKJV).

"Behold, we are going up to Jerusalem, and the Son of Man will be betrayed to the chief priests and to the scribes; and they will condemn Him to death and deliver Him to the Gentiles; and they will mock Him, and scourge Him, and spit on Him, and kill Him. And the third day He will rise again" (Mark 10:33–34 NKJV).

"Now as they said these things, Jesus Himself stood in the midst of them, and said to them, 'Peace to you.' But they were terrified and frightened, and supposed they had seen a spirit. And He said to them, 'Why are you troubled? And why do doubts arise in your hearts? Behold My hands and My feet, that it is I Myself. Handle Me and see, for a spirit does not have flesh and bones as you see I have'" (Luke 24:36–39 NKJV).

"Now if we have died with Christ, we believe that we shall also live with Him, knowing that Christ, having been raised from the dead, is never to die again; death no longer is master over Him. For the death that He died, He died to sin once for all; but the life that He lives, He lives to God. Even so consider yourselves to be dead to sin, but alive to God in Christ Jesus" (Romans 6:8–11 NASB).

"For I delivered to you first of all that which I also received: that Christ died for our sins according to the Scriptures, and that He was buried, and that He rose again the third day according to the Scriptures, and that He was seen by Cephas, then by the twelve. After that He was seen by over five hundred brethren at once, of whom the greater part remain to the present, but some have fallen asleep. After that He was seen by James, then by all the apostles. Then last of all He was seen by me also" (1 Corinthians 15:3–8 NKJV). Note: This was written by the apostle Paul.

"What is the surpassing greatness of His power toward us who believe. These are in accordance with the working of the strength of His might which He brought about in Christ, when He raised Him from the dead and seated Him at His right hand in the heavenly places, far above all rule and authority and power and dominion, and every name that is named, not only in this age but also in the one to come" (Ephesians 1:19–21 NASB).

"Fixing our eyes on Jesus, the author and perfecter of faith, who for the joy set before Him endured the cross, despising the shame, and has sat down at the right hand of the throne of God" (Hebrews 12:2 NASB).

"He indeed was foreordained before the foundation of the world, but was manifest in these last times for you who through Him believe in God, who raised Him from the dead and gave Him glory, so that your faith and hope are in God" (1 Peter 1:20–21 NKJV).

Chapter 32

JESUS IS GOD

Jesus said to them, "Most assuredly, I say to you, before Abraham was, I AM" (John 8:58 NKJV). This is a powerful statement made by Jesus, revealing that He is God by confirming that He (before His human birth) existed before Abraham, and by making the statement, "I AM."

Let's read Exodus 3:14 (NKJV): "And God said to Moses, 'I AM WHO I AM.' And He said, 'Thus you shall say to the children of Israel, "I AM has sent me to you."'"3

From Exodus, you can see the connection that "I AM" is God and "I AM" is Jesus. They are the same.

"In the beginning was the Word, and the Word was with God, and the Word was God. . . . All things were made through Him, and without Him nothing was made that was made. . . . He was in the world, and the world was made through Him, and the world did not know Him. . . . And the Word became flesh and dwelt among us, and we beheld His glory, the glory as of the only begotten of the Father, full of grace and truth" (John 1:1, 3, 10, 14 NKJV).

"So Jesus said, 'When you lift up the Son of Man, then you will know that I am He, and I do nothing on My own initiative, but I speak these things as the Father taught Me. And He who sent Me is with Me; He has not left Me alone, for I always do the things that are pleasing to Him'" (John 8:28–29 NASB).

"I and the Father are One" (John 10:30 AMP).

"Then Jesus cried out and said, 'He who believes in Me, believes not in Me but in Him who sent Me. And he who sees Me sees Him who sent Me'" (John 12:44–45 NKJV).

"He who has seen Me has seen the Father; so how can you say, 'Show us the Father'? Do you not believe that I am in the Father, and the Father in Me? The words that I speak to you I do not speak on My own authority; but the Father who dwells in Me does the works" (John 14:9–10 NKJV).

"Let this same attitude and purpose and [humble] mind be in you which was in Christ Jesus: [Let Him be your example in humility:] who, although being essentially one with God and in the form of God [possessing the fullness of the attributes which make God God], did not think this equality with God was a thing to be eagerly grasped or retained, but stripped Himself [of all privileges and rightful dignity], so as to assume the guise of a servant (slave), in that He became like men and was born a human being. And after He had appeared in human form, He abased and humbled Himself [still further] and carried His obedience to the extreme of death, even the death of the cross!" (Philippians 2:5–8 AMP).

"Christ is the visible image of the invisible God. He existed before anything was created and is supreme over all creation" (Colossians 1:15 NLT).

Chapter 33

JUDGE NOT

> Only a kind person is able to judge another justly and to make
> allowances for his weaknesses. A kind eye, while recognizing
> defects, sees beyond them.
> —Lawrence G. Lovasik

J udge not" does not mean that we should never judge. If so, we
would have to throw out our court system. People make judgments
every day in our courts.

What the Bible says is that when we judge, we must use God's
Word to discern the situation and judge righteously. Look beyond the
personal appearance of the man and look at the man's actions. When
we look at his actions and gain insight through facts and searching for
the truth, we will be able to discern or judge properly.

I know that in my daily life I am guilty of judging another person,
only to realize I have the same fault I am seeing in him. It is so easy to
make snap judgments, but next time, wait. Sift through the information and come to a godly conclusion.

"If you judge, investigate."
—Lucius Annaeus Seneca, Roman philosopher

"Do not judge, or you too will be judged. For in the same way you judge others, you will be judged, and with the measure you use, it will be measured to you" (Matthew 7:1–2 NIV).

"Judge not, and you will not be judged; condemn not, and you will not be condemned" (Luke 6:37 ESV).

"Stop judging by mere appearances, and make a right judgment" (John 7:24 NIV).

"Therefore you have no excuse or defense or justification, O man, whoever you are who judges and condemns another. For in posing as judge and passing sentence on another, you condemn yourself, because you who judge are habitually practicing the very same things [that you censure and denounce]" (Romans 2:1 AMP).

"You, then, why do you judge your brother? Or why do you look down on your brother? For we will all stand before God's judgment seat" (Romans 14:10 NIV).

"So then each of us will give an account of himself to God. Therefore let us not pass judgment on one another any longer, but rather decide never to put a stumbling block or hindrance in the way of a brother" (Romans 14:12–13 ESV).

Chapter 34

JUSTICE, JUDGING, AND JUDGMENT

Man is unjust, but God is just, and finally justice triumphs.
—Henry Wadsworth Longfellow, *Evangeline*

There will be a final judgment. God will be the One to judge. In our court system, sometimes the jury may arrive at a guilty verdict for a sex offender, only to have the judge give the convicted person probation for six months. Our response is, "Where's the justice?" In our eyes, the punishment does not fit the crime. Unfortunately, we may not see justice during our lifetime, but God is the final judge. God knows who is guilty, and the guilty person will not escape His judgment.

"The LORD judges the peoples; judge me, O LORD, according to my righteousness and according to the integrity that is in me" (Psalm 7:8 ESV).

"God is an honest judge. He is angry with the wicked every day" (Psalm 7:11 NLT).

"But the LORD shall remain and continue forever; He has prepared and established His throne for judgment. And He will judge the world in righteousness (rightness and equity); He will minister justice to the peoples in uprightness" (Psalm 9:7–8 AMP).

"For the LORD will judge His people and have compassion on His servants" (Deuteronomy 32:36 NKJV).

"Then shall the trees of the wood sing out for joy before the LORD, for He comes to judge and govern the earth" (1 Chronicles 16:33 AMP).

"For great is the wrath of the LORD that is poured out on us, because our fathers have not kept the word of the LORD, to do according to all that is written in this book" (2 Chronicles 34:21 NKJV). Note: Second Chronicles 34:14–19 states that the book of the Law of God given by Moses was read to King Josiah of Judah, and this was King Josiah's response.

"Let the peoples praise You, O God; let all the peoples praise You. Oh, let the nations be glad and sing for joy! For You shall judge the people righteously, and govern the nations on earth. Selah" (Psalm 67:3–4 NKJV).

"But it is God who judges: He brings one down, he exalts another" (Psalm 75:7 NIV).

"Say among the nations that the LORD reigns; the world also is established, so that it cannot be moved; He shall judge and rule the people righteously and with justice" (Psalm 96:10 AMP).

"Be afraid of the sword, for wrath brings the punishment of the sword, that you may know there is a judgment" (Job 19:29 ESV).

"If I have walked with falsehood and my foot has hastened to deceit; (Let me be weighed in a just balance, and let God know my integrity!)" (Job 31:5–6 ESV).

"If I have made gold my trust and hope or have said to fine gold, You are my confidence, if I rejoiced because my wealth was great and because my [powerful] hand [alone] had gotten much, if I beheld [as an object of worship] the sunlight when it shone or the moon walking in its brightness, and my heart has been secretly enticed by them or my mouth has kissed my hand [in homage to them], this also would have been [a heinous and principal] iniquity to demand the judges' action and punishment, for I would have denied and been false to the God who is above" (Job 31:24–28 AMP).

"The conclusion, when all has been heard, is: fear God and keep His commandments, because this applies to every person. For God will bring every act to judgment, everything which is hidden, whether it is good or evil" (Ecclesiastes 12:13–14 NASB).

"He is the LORD our God; His judgments are in all the earth. He has remembered His covenant forever, the word which He commanded to a thousand generations" (Psalm 105:7–8 NASB).

"I will utter My judgments against them concerning all their wickedness, because they have forsaken Me, burned incense to other gods, and worshiped the works of their own hands" (Jeremiah 1:16 NKJV).

"I will deal with them according to their conduct, and by their own standards I will judge them. Then they will know that I am the LORD" (Ezekiel 7:27 NIV).

"Upright are Your judgments" (Psalm 119:137 NKJV).

"And every one of Your righteous judgments endures forever" (Psalm 119:160 NKJV).

"For the LORD will judge His people and will have compassion on His servants" (Psalm 135:14 NASB).

"Therefore having overlooked the times of ignorance, God is now declaring to men that all people everywhere should repent, because He has fixed a day in which He will judge the world in righteousness through a Man whom He has appointed, having furnished proof to all men by raising Him from the dead" (Acts 17:30–31 NASB).

"But we know that the judgment of God is according to truth" (Romans 2:2 NKJV).

"On that day when, according to my gospel, God judges the secrets of men by Christ Jesus" (Romans 2:16 ESV).

"God and of Christ Jesus, who is to judge the living and the dead, and by His appearing and His kingdom" (2 Timothy 4:1 NASB).

"God will surely judge people who are immoral and those who commit adultery" (Hebrews 13:4 NLT).

Chapter 35

LIGHT

Now I'm so happy, no sorrow in sight
Praise the Lord, I saw the light
—Hank Williams, "I Saw the Light"

You walk into a dark room and you bump into walls, furniture, and finally a lamp. You turn the switch on the lamp, and there is light! You can see!

God is waiting to turn your light on so you can step out of the darkness. God's Word can illuminate you so that you can shine for all to experience.

"Even in darkness light dawns for the upright, for the gracious and compassionate and righteous man" (Psalm 112:4 NIV).

"If you pour yourself out for the hungry and satisfy the desire of the afflicted, then shall your light rise in the darkness and your gloom be as the noonday. And the LORD will guide you continually and satisfy your desire in scorched places and make your bones strong; and you shall be like a watered garden, like a spring of water, whose waters do not fail" (Isaiah 58:10–11 ESV).

"The sun shall be no more your light by day, nor for brightness shall the moon give you light; but the LORD will be your everlasting light, and your God will be your glory" (Isaiah 60:19 ESV).

"This is the verdict: Light has come into the world, but men loved darkness instead of light because their deeds were evil. Everyone who does evil hates the light, and will not come into the light for fear that his deeds will be exposed. But whoever lives by the truth comes into the light, so that it may be seen plainly that what he has done has been done through God" (John 3:19–21 NIV).

"Then Jesus again spoke to them, saying, 'I am the Light of the world; he who follows Me will not walk in the darkness, but will have the Light of life'" (John 8:12 NASB).

"I have come as a Light into the world, so that whoever believes in Me [whoever cleaves to and trusts in and relies on Me] may not continue to live in darkness" (John 12:46 AMP).

"For you were once darkness, but now you are light in the Lord. Live as children of light (for the fruit of the light consists in all goodness, righteousness and truth) and find out what pleases the Lord. Have nothing to do with the fruitless deeds of darkness, but rather expose them" (Ephesians 5:8–11 NIV).

"Therefore He says: 'Awake, you who sleep, arise from the dead, and Christ will give you light'" (Ephesians 5:14 NKJV).

"Do all things without grumbling or disputing; so that you will prove yourselves to be blameless and innocent, children of God above reproach in the midst of a crooked and perverse generation, among whom you appear as lights in the world, holding fast the word of life, so that in the day of Christ I will have reason to glory because I did not run in vain nor toil in vain" (Philippians 2:14–16 NASB).

"Your word is a lamp to my feet and a light to my path" (Psalm 119:105 AMP).

Chapter 36

LOVE

The ultimate lesson all of us have to learn is unconditional love,
which includes not only others but ourselves as well.
—Elisabeth Kubler-Ross, Swiss-American psychiatrist and author

There's romantic love and there's unconditional love. Romantic love can end, but unconditional love is infinite. That is God's love for you. No matter what you do, God still loves *you*.

Immersing yourself in God's unconditional love changes your heart, attitude, and direction in life. It can be a magical transformation from the *old* you to a *new* you.

Tell of the cross where they nailed Him,
Writhing in anguish and pain;
Tell of the grave where they laid Him,
Tell how He liveth again.
Love in that story so tender,
Clearer than ever I see;
Stay, let me weep while you whisper,
"Love paid the ransom for me."
—Frances J. Crosby, "Tell Me the Story of Jesus"

"Let those who love the LORD hate evil" (Psalm 97:10 NIV).

"Consider how I love Your precepts; revive me, O LORD, according to Your lovingkindness" (Psalm 119:159 NKJV).

"Many waters cannot quench love, neither can floods drown it" (Solomon 8:7 AMP).

"A new commandment I give to you, that you love one another, even as I have loved you, that you also love one another. By this all men will know that you are My disciples, if you have love for one another" (John 13:34–35 NASB).

"And we know that all things work together for good to those who love God, to those who are the called according to His purpose" (Romans 8:28 NKJV).

"Yet in all these things we are more than conquerors through Him who loved us. For I am persuaded that neither death nor life, nor angels nor principalities nor powers, nor things present nor things to come, nor height nor depth, nor any other created thing, shall be able to separate us from the love of God which is in Christ Jesus our Lord" (Romans 8:37–39 NKJV).

"Let love be genuine" (Romans 12:9 ESV).

"Owe nothing to anyone—except for your obligation to love one another. If you love your neighbor, you will fulfill the requirements of God's law" (Romans 13:8 NLT).

"'You shall love your neighbor as yourself.' Love does no wrong to a neighbor; therefore love is the fulfilling of the law" (Romans 13:9–10 ESV).

"We know that 'all of us possess knowledge.' This 'knowledge' puffs up, but love builds up. If anyone imagines that he knows something, he does not yet know as he ought to know. But if anyone loves God, he is known by God" (1 Corinthians 8:1–3 ESV).

"If I speak with the tongues of men and of angels, but do not have love, I have become a noisy gong or a clanging cymbal. If I have the gift of prophecy, and know all mysteries and all knowledge; and if I have all faith, so as to remove mountains, but do not have love, I am nothing. And if I give all my possessions to feed the poor, and if I surrender my body to be burned, but do not have love, it profits me nothing" (1 Corinthians 13:1–3 NASB).

"And now these three remain: faith, hope and love. But the greatest of these is love" (1 Corinthians 13:13 NIV).

"Be on your guard; stand firm in the faith; be men of courage; be strong. Do everything in love" (1 Corinthians 16:13–14 NIV).

"For you were called to freedom, brethren; only do not turn your freedom into an opportunity for the flesh, but through love serve one another. For the whole Law is fulfilled in one word, in the statement, 'You shall love your neighbor as yourself.' But if you bite and devour one another, take care that you are not consumed by one another" (Galatians 5:13–15 NASB).

"And walk in love, as Christ also has loved us and given Himself for us, an offering and a sacrifice to God" (Ephesians 5:2 NKJV).

"And above all these put on love, which binds everything together in perfect harmony" (Colossians 3:14 ESV).

"For God is not unrighteous to forget or overlook your labor and the love which you have shown for His name's sake" (Hebrews 6:10 AMP).

"Love one another fervently from a pure heart" (1 Peter 1:22 AMP).

"And above all things have fervent love for one another, for 'love will cover a multitude of sins'" (1 Peter 4:8 NKJV).

"Beloved, let us love one another, for love is from God, and whoever loves has been born of God and knows God. Anyone who does not love does not know God, because God is love" (1 John 4:7–8 ESV).

"There is no fear in love; but perfect love casteth out fear: because fear hath torment. He that feareth is not made perfect in love" (1 John 4:18 KJV).

Chapter 37

MARRIAGE AND FAMILY

There's a family Bible on the table
Each page is torn and hard to read
—Willy Nelson, "Family Bible"

Do families have a "family" Bible or even read the Bible together in their homes? I have a one-hundred-year-old friend who remembers her dad reading the Bible to her family around the kitchen table. I don't remember it happening in my family and oh, how I wish it had.

Following God's wisdom will save marriages, improve parenting, give direction to children, and make the family more cohesive. Will there be difficult moments? Absolutely, but following God's instructions will make the difficult moments bearable and achievable and provide a calm in the midst of the storm.

Children look to their parents for guidance. You are your child's role model. God is your role model. Teach your children well.

Tell me the story of Jesus,
Write on my heart every word
Tell me the story most precious,
Sweetest that ever was heard.
—Frances J. Crosby, "Tell Me the Story of Jesus"

Husband and Wife

"But at the beginning of creation God 'made them male and female.' 'For this reason a man will leave his father and mother and be united to his wife, and the two will become one flesh.' So they are no longer two, but one. Therefore what God has joined together, let man not separate" (Mark 10:6–9 NIV).

"But because of the temptation to sexual immorality, each man should have his own wife and each woman her own husband. The husband should give to his wife her conjugal rights, and likewise the wife to her husband. For the wife does not have authority over her own body, but the husband does. Likewise the husband does not have authority over his own body, but the wife does. Do not deprive one another, except perhaps by agreement for a limited time, that you may devote yourselves to prayer; but then come together again, so that Satan may not tempt you because of your lack of self-control" (1 Corinthians 7:2–5 ESV).

"Are you married? Do not seek a divorce" (1 Corinthians 7:27 NIV).

"A wife is bound to her husband as long as he lives. If her husband dies, she is free to marry anyone she wishes, but only if he loves the Lord. But in my opinion it would be better for her to stay single" (1 Corinthians 7:39–40 NLT).

"Wives, submit to your husbands, as is fitting in the Lord. Husbands, love your wives, and do not be harsh with them" (Colossians 3:18–19 ESV).

"If anyone does not provide for his relatives, and especially for his immediate family, he has denied the faith and is worse than an unbeliever" (1 Timothy 5:8 NIV).

"Better to live in a desert than with a quarrelsome and ill-tempered wife" (Proverbs 21:19 NIV).

"In the same way you married men should live considerately with [your wives], with an intelligent recognition [of the marriage relation], honoring the woman as [physically] the weaker, but [realizing that you] are joint heirs of the grace (God's unmerited favor) of life, in order that your prayers may not be hindered and cut off. [Otherwise you cannot pray effectively.]" (1 Peter 3:7 AMP).

"Who can find a virtuous woman? for her price is far above rubies" (Proverbs 31:10 KJV).

Parents

"If you refuse to discipline your son, it proves you don't love him; for if you love him you will be prompt to punish him" (Proverbs 13:24 TLB).

"Discipline your son, for in that there is hope; do not be a willing party to his death" (Proverbs 19:18 NIV).

"A youngster's heart is filled with rebellion, but punishment will drive it out of him" (Proverbs 22:15 TLB).

"Don't fail to discipline your children. They won't die if you spank them. Physical discipline may well save them from death" (Proverbs 23:13–14 NLT).

"Fathers, do not provoke your children to anger by the way you treat them. Rather, bring them up with the discipline and instruction that comes from the Lord" (Ephesians 6:4 NLT).

"Fathers, do not provoke your children, lest they become discouraged" (Colossians 3:21 ESV).

"Scolding and spanking a child helps him to learn. Left to himself, he brings shame to his mother" (Proverbs 29:15 TLB).

"Discipline your children, and they will give you peace of mind and will make your heart glad" (Proverbs 29:17 NLT).

"For the moment all discipline seems painful rather than pleasant, but later it yields the peaceful fruit of righteousness to those who have been trained by it" (Hebrews 12:11 ESV).

Children

"Each of you shall give due respect to his mother and his father, and keep My Sabbaths holy. I the LORD am your God" (Leviticus 19:3 AMP).

"My child, don't reject the LORD's discipline, and don't be upset when he corrects you. For the LORD corrects those he loves, just as a father corrects a child in whom he delights" (Proverbs 3:11–12 NLT).

"He who heeds discipline shows the way to life, but whoever ignores correction leads others astray" (Proverbs 10:17 NIV).

"Only a fool despises a parent's discipline; whoever learns from correction is wise" (Proverbs 15:5 NLT).

"A foolish child brings disaster to a father" (Proverbs 19:13 NCV).

"Children who mistreat their father or chase away their mother are an embarrassment and a public disgrace" (Proverbs 19:26 NLT).

"If you stop listening to instruction, my child, you will turn your back on knowledge" (Proverbs 19:27 NLT).

"Even a child is known by his actions, by whether his conduct is pure and right" (Proverbs 20:11 NIV).

"Whoever curses his father or his mother, his lamp shall be put out in complete darkness" (Proverbs 20:20 AMP).

"My son, if your heart is wise, my heart will be glad, even mine; yes, my heart will rejoice when your lips speak right things" (Proverbs 23:15–16 AMP).

"My child, listen and be wise: Keep your heart on the right course. Do not carouse with drunkards or feast with gluttons, for they are on their way to poverty, and too much sleep clothes them in rags" (Proverbs 23:19–21 NLT).

"Listen to your father, who gave you life, and don't despise your mother when she is old" (Proverbs 23:22 NLT).

"The father of godly children has cause for joy. What a pleasure to have children who are wise. So give your father and mother joy! May she who gave you birth be happy" (Proverbs 23:24–25 NLT).

"My son, give me your heart and let your eyes observe and delight in my ways" (Proverbs 23:26 AMP).

"Be wise, my child, and make my heart glad. Then I will be able to answer my critics" (Proverbs 27:11 NLT).

"Children, obey your parents in the Lord, for this is right. 'Honor your father and mother,' which is the first commandment with promise: 'that it may be well with you and you may live long on the earth'" (Ephesians 6:1–3 NKJV).

"Children, obey your parents in everything, for this pleases the Lord" (Colossians 3:20 ESV).

"But if she has children or grandchildren, their first responsibility is to show godliness at home and repay their parents by taking care of them. This is something that pleases God" (1 Timothy 5:4 NLT).

Chapter 38

MERCY

D o you have the gift of mercy? If you do, you have a heartfelt compassion to help one who is in misery. It is a wonderful gift to be sensitive to a person's need and to desire to help him get through a troublesome time. During this person's troubles, be sure to give only the help that will be beneficial to him. Be cautious that you don't become a crutch for the person.

Sometimes, we want so much to help relieve the person of his pain that we interfere with God's plan for the person. Unfortunately, we may be hindering the person, keeping him from growing from this situation and prolonging his troubles. God did not put us on earth to fix every problem.

Then how do we know how much help to give? This is the time that you ask God for wisdom for what to do.

> God, give us grace to accept with serenity
> the things that cannot be changed,
> courage to change the things which should be changed,
> and the wisdom to distinguish the one from the other.
> —Reinhold Niebuhr, "Serenity Prayer"

"But showing mercy and steadfast love to a thousand generations of those who love Me and keep My commandments" (Exodus 20:6 AMP).

"And David said to Gad, I am in great distress. Let us fall into the hands of the LORD, for His mercies are many and great; but let me not fall into the hands of man" (2 Samuel 24:14 AMP).

"O give thanks to the LORD, for He is good; for His mercy and loving-kindness endure forever!" (1 Chronicles 16:34 AMP).

"For He is good, for His mercy endures forever" (2 Chronicles 5:13 NKJV).

"Give thanks to the LORD, for His mercy and loving-kindness endure forever!" (2 Chronicles 20:21 AMP).

"Let the wicked forsake his way and the unrighteous man his thoughts; and let him return to the LORD, and He will have love, pity, and mercy for him, and to our God, for He will multiply to him His abundant pardon" (Isaiah 55:7 AMP).

"This I recall to my mind, therefore I have hope. Through the LORD's mercies we are not consumed, because His compassions fail not" (Lamentations 3:21–22 NKJV).

"O LORD, great and awesome God, who keeps His covenant and mercy with those who love Him, and with those who keep His commandments" (Daniel 9:4 NKJV).

"His mercy is upon generation after generation toward those who fear him" (Luke 1:50 NASB).

"Be merciful to me, LORD, for I am faint; O LORD, heal me, for my bones are in agony" (Psalm 6:2 NIV).

"All the paths of the LORD are mercy and truth" (Psalm 25:10 NKJV).

"Hear, O LORD, and be merciful to me! O LORD, be my helper!" (Psalm 30:10 ESV).

"I will be glad and rejoice in Your mercy and steadfast love, because You have seen my affliction, You have taken note of my life's distresses" (Psalm 31:7 AMP).

"Be merciful to me, O LORD, for I am in distress; my eyes grow weak with sorrow, my soul and my body with grief" (Psalm 31:9 NIV).

"But love your enemies, do good, and lend, hoping for nothing in return; and your reward will be great, and you will be sons of the Most High. For He is kind to the unthankful and evil. Therefore be merciful, just as your Father also is merciful" (Luke 6:35–36 NKJV).

"We have different gifts, according to the grace given us. . . . If it is showing mercy, let him do it cheerfully" (Romans 12:6, 8 NIV).

"He who oppresses the poor reproaches, mocks, and insults his Maker, but he who is kind and merciful to the needy honors Him" (Proverbs 14:31 AMP).

"Have mercy upon me, O God, according to Your steadfast love; according to the multitude of Your tender mercy and loving-kindness blot out my transgressions. Wash me thoroughly [and repeatedly] from my iniquity and guilt and cleanse me and make me wholly pure from my sin! For I am conscious of my transgressions and I acknowledge them; my sin is ever before me" (Psalm 51:1–3 AMP).

"Be merciful to me, O God, be merciful to me! For my soul trusts in You; and in the shadow of Your wings I will make my refuge, until these calamities have passed by. I will cry out to God Most High, to God who performs all things for me. He shall send from heaven and save me; He reproaches the one who would swallow me up. Selah God shall send forth His mercy and His truth" (Psalm 57:1–3 NKJV).

"But I will sing of Your power; yes, I will sing aloud of your mercy in the morning; for You have been my defense and refuge in the day of my trouble. To You, O my Strength, I will sing praises; for God is my defense, my God of mercy" (Psalm 59:16–17 NKJV).

"Also to You, O LORD, belong mercy and loving-kindness, for You render to every man according to his work" (Psalm 62:12 AMP).

"Come and hear, all you who fear God, and I will declare what He has done for my soul. I cried to Him with my mouth, and He was extolled with my tongue. If I regard iniquity in my heart, the Lord will not hear. But certainly God has heard me; He has attended to the voice of my prayer. Blessed be God, who has not turned away my prayer, nor His mercy from me!" (Psalm 66:16–20 NKJV).

"For You, O Lord, are good, and ready to forgive [our trespasses, sending them away, letting them go completely and forever]; and You are abundant in mercy and loving-kindness to all those who call upon You" (Psalm 86:5 AMP).

"I will praise You, O Lord my God, with all my heart, and I will glorify Your name forevermore. For great is Your mercy toward me, and You have delivered my soul from the depths of Sheol" (Psalm 86:12–13 NKJV). Note: *Sheol* is Hades.

"Mercy and loving-kindness and truth go before Your face" (Psalm 89:14 AMP).

"When I said, My foot is slipping, Your mercy and loving-kindness, O Lord, held me up" (Psalm 94:18 AMP).

"His mercy is everlasting" (Psalm 100:5 NKJV).

"The Lord is merciful and gracious, slow to anger, and abounding in mercy" (Psalm 103:8 NKJV).

"But the mercy of the Lord is from everlasting to everlasting on those who fear Him, and His righteousness to children's children, to such as keep His covenant, and to those who remember His commandments to do them" (Psalm 103:17–18 NKJV).

"The Lord is gracious and righteous; our God is full of compassion" (Psalm 116:5 NIV).

"But when the kindness of God our Savior and His love for mankind appeared, He saved us, not on the basis of deeds which we have done in righteousness, but according to His mercy" (Titus 3:4–5 NASB).

"Let Your tender mercy and loving-kindness come to me that I may live, for Your law is my delight!" (Psalm 119:77 AMP).

"Unto You I lift up my eyes, O You who dwell in the heavens. Behold, as the eyes of servants look to the hand of their masters, as the eyes of a maid to the hand of her mistress, so our eyes look to the LORD our God, until He has mercy on us. Have mercy on us, O LORD, have mercy on us! For we are exceedingly filled with contempt. Our soul is exceedingly filled with the scorn of those who are at ease, with the contempt of the proud" (Psalm 123:1–4 NKJV).

"O give thanks to the LORD of lords, for His mercy and loving-kindness endure forever—to Him who alone does great wonders, for His mercy and loving-kindness endure forever" (Psalm 136:3–4 AMP).

Chapter 39

OBEDIENCE

Obey God and leave all the consequences to Him.
—Dr. Charles Stanley

We know that if we do not obey the stop sign when we are driving, we could be in an accident or get a ticket. If we do not obey the rules of the game, we will be penalized or ejected from the game. There are consequences for not obeying the rules.

If we want to be blessed, then we must obey God. To obey God, we have to read His Word to know how He wants us to respond. If we do, we will experience God's love and blessings every day. It may be a small blessing, like finding a parking space close to the entrance of a building, or a huge blessing, like an unexpected financial windfall.

I have heard people say they are doing fine without the Bible. They are happy with their lives. And I say that if you *haven't* obeyed God and you think you are happy, you *don't* know what happy is. Obey God and be amazed!

"You shall therefore love the LORD your God, and always keep His charge, His statutes, His ordinances, and His commandments" (Deuteronomy 11:1 NASB).

"When Jacob had gone into Egypt, and your fathers cried out to the LORD, then the LORD sent Moses and Aaron, who brought your fathers out of Egypt and made them dwell in this place. And when they forgot the LORD their God, He sold them into the hand of Sisera, commander of the army of Hazor, into the hand of the Philistines, and into the hand of the king of Moab; and they fought against them. Then they cried out to the LORD, and said, 'We have sinned, because we have forsaken the LORD and served the Baals and Ashtoreths; but now deliver us from the hand of our enemies, and we will serve You.' And the LORD sent Jerubbaal, Bedan, Jephthah, and Samuel, and delivered you out of the hand of your enemies on every side; and you dwelt in safety" (1 Samuel 12:8–11 NKJV). Note: Baal was the chief god of the Canaanites. Ashtoreth was a goddess of the Sidonians. The Israelites had worshiped idols of Baal and Ashtoreth.

"Samuel said to Saul, 'You have acted foolishly; you have not kept the commandment of the LORD your God, which He commanded you, for now the LORD would have established your kingdom over Israel forever. But now your kingdom shall not endure. The LORD has sought out for Himself a man after His own heart, and the LORD has appointed him as ruler over His people, because you have not kept what the LORD commanded you'" (1 Samuel 13:13–14 NASB).

"Behold, to obey is better than sacrifice. . . . For rebellion is as the sin of witchcraft, and stubbornness is as iniquity and idolatry, because you have rejected the word of the LORD, He also has rejected you from being king" (1 Samuel 15:22–23 NKJV).

"So Saul died for his breach of faith. He broke faith with the LORD in that he did not keep the command of the LORD, and also consulted a medium, seeking guidance" (1 Chronicles 10:13 ESV). Note: Saul was the first king of Israel.

"But He knows the way I take; when He has tried me, I shall come forth as gold. My foot has held fast to His path; I have kept His way and not turned aside. I have not departed from the command of His lips; I have treasured the words of His mouth more than my necessary food" (Job 23:10–12 NASB).

"He also opens their ear to instruction, and commands that they turn from iniquity. If they obey and serve Him, they shall spend their days in prosperity, and their years in pleasures" (Job 36:10–11 NKJV).

"Direct my steps by Your word, and let no iniquity have dominion over me" (Psalm 119:133 NKJV).

"If you are willing and obedient, you will eat the best from the land" (Isaiah 1:19 NIV).

"Therefore, as the tongue of fire devours the stubble, and as dry grass sinks down in the flame, so their root will be as rottenness, and their blossom go up like dust; for they have rejected the law of the LORD of hosts, and have despised the word of the Holy One of Israel" (Isaiah 5:24 ESV).

"For I did not speak on My own initiative, but the Father Himself who sent Me has given Me a commandment as to what to say and what to speak. I know that His commandment is eternal life; therefore the things I speak, I speak just as the Father has told Me" (John 12:49–50 NASB).

"But Peter and the apostles answered, 'We must obey God rather than men. The God of our fathers raised up Jesus, whom you had put to death by hanging Him on a cross. He is the one whom God exalted to His right hand as a Prince and a Savior, to grant repentance to Israel, and forgiveness of sins. And we are witnesses of these things; and so is the Holy Spirit, whom God has given to those who obey Him'" (Acts 5:29–32 NASB).

"Therefore, in the present case I advise you: Leave these men alone! Let them go! For if their purpose or activity is of human origin, it will fail. But if it is from God, you will not be able to stop these men; you will only find yourselves fighting against God" (Acts 5:38–39 NIV).

"Slaves, obey your earthly masters in everything; and do it, not only when their eye is on you and to win their favor, but with sincerity of heart and reverence for the Lord. Whatever you do, work at it with all your heart, as working for the Lord, not for men, since you know that you will receive an inheritance from the Lord as a reward. It is the Lord Christ you are serving" (Colossians 3:22–24 NIV).

"Today, if you would hear His voice and when you hear it, do not harden your hearts" (Hebrews 4:7 AMP).

"Although He was a Son, He learned obedience from the things which He suffered. And having been made perfect, He became to all those who obey Him the source of eternal salvation" (Hebrews 5:8–9 NASB). Note: This passage is speaking about Jesus.

Chapter 40

OMNIPOTENT GOD

O Lord my God, when I in awesome wonder,
Consider all the worlds Thy hands have made.
—Carl Gustav Boberg, "How Great Thou Art"

Our minds cannot comprehend our all-powerful God. God will orchestrate the return of Jesus, the binding and throwing of Satan into a bottomless pit, and the reign of God over the world.

"For great is the LORD and greatly to be praised; He is to be feared above all gods. For all the gods of the peoples are idols, but the LORD made the heavens. Splendor and majesty are before Him, strength and beauty are in His sanctuary" (Psalm 96:4–6 NASB).

"Bless the LORD, O my soul; and all that is within me, bless His holy name! Bless the LORD, O my soul, and forget not all His benefits: who forgives all your iniquities, who heals all your diseases, who redeems your life from destruction, who crowns you with lovingkindness and tender mercies, who satisfies your mouth with good things, so that your youth is renewed like the eagle's" (Psalm 103:1–5 NKJV).

"Trust in the LORD forever, for the LORD GOD is an everlasting rock" (Isaiah 26:4 ESV).

"And there is no other God besides Me, a righteous God and a Savior; there is none except Me" (Isaiah 45:21 NASB).

"But My salvation will be forever, and My righteousness will not wane" (Isaiah 51:6 NASB).

"Therefore behold, I am going to make them know—this time I will make them know My power and My might; and they shall know that My name is the LORD" (Jeremiah 16:21 NASB).

"For He is the living God, and steadfast forever; His kingdom is the one which shall not be destroyed, and his dominion shall endure to the end" (Daniel 6:26 NKJV).

"For I am the LORD, I do not change" (Malachi 3:6 AMP).

"You, LORD, in the beginning laid the foundation of the earth, and the heavens are the work of Your hands. They will perish, but You remain; and they will all grow old like a garment; like a cloak You will fold them up, and they will be changed. But You are the same, and Your years will not fail" (Hebrews 1:10–12 NKJV).

"I know that the LORD is great, that our LORD is greater than all gods. The LORD does whatever pleases him, in the heavens and on the earth, in the seas and all their depths" (Psalm 135:5–6 NIV).

"'I am the Alpha and the Omega,' says the Lord God, 'who is, and who was, and who is to come, the Almighty'" (Revelation 1:8 NIV).

Chapter 41

OMNISCIENT GOD

Did you wonder as a child if you had psychic parents? Did they seem to know what you were up to before you did it?

God is like that. He knows all our thoughts—spoken or not. He knows how we feel. He knows our weaknesses and our strengths. We can hide nothing from Him.

"For the LORD searches all hearts and understands every plan and thought" (1 Chronicles 28:9 ESV).

"But He knew their thoughts and said to them, 'Any kingdom divided against itself is laid waste; and a house divided against itself falls'" (Luke 11:17 NASB).

"O LORD, You have searched me and known me. You know my sitting down and my rising up; You understand my thought afar off. You comprehend my path and my lying down, and are acquainted with all my ways. For there is not a word on my tongue, but behold, O LORD, You know it altogether" (Psalm 139:1–4 NKJV).

"The eyes of the LORD are in every place, keeping watch upon the evil and the good" (Proverbs 15:3 AMP).

"Nothing is covered up that will not be revealed, or hidden that will not be known. Therefore whatever you have said in the dark shall be heard in the light, and what you have whispered in private rooms shall be proclaimed on the housetops" (Luke 12:2–3 ESV).

"For the word of God is living and active. Sharper than any double-edged sword, it penetrates even to dividing soul and spirit, joints and marrow; it judges the thoughts and attitudes of the heart" (Hebrews 4:12 NIV).

"And there is no creature hidden from His sight, but all things are naked and open to the eyes of Him to whom we must give account" (Hebrews 4:13 NKJV).

"For whenever our heart condemns us, God is greater than our heart, and he knows everything" (1 John 3:20 ESV).

Chapter 42

OUR ROCK, STRENGTH, REFUGE, AND MIGHTY FORTRESS

Say to the LORD: "My refuge, My Rock in whom I trust!"
And He will raise you up on eagle's wings.
—Michael Joncas, "On Eagle's Wings"

Thank You, God, for allowing us to turn our burdens over to You. When we face a challenging situation—surgery, a failing marriage, the death of a child, our own death, or the challenge of being truthful in a difficult situation—You are our strength. Our friends can't do it for us, but You wrap Your arms around us and get us through the challenges.

Rely on God and remember His words: "I will never leave you nor forsake you" (Hebrews 13:5 NKJV).

"The LORD is my rock and my fortress and my deliverer; the God of my strength, in whom I will trust; my shield and the horn of my salvation, my stronghold and my refuge; my Savior, You save me from violence. I will call upon the LORD, who is worthy to be praised; so shall I be saved from my enemies" (2 Samuel 22:2–4 NKJV).

"For who is God, except the LORD? And who is a rock, except our God? God is my strength and power, and He makes my way perfect. He makes my feet like the feet of deer, and sets me on my high places" (2 Samuel 22:32–34 NKJV).

"Then David said to Solomon his son, 'Be strong and courageous and do it. Do not be afraid and do not be dismayed, for the LORD God, even my God, is with you. He will not leave you or forsake you, until all the work for the service of the house of the LORD is finished'" (1 Chronicles 28:20 ESV).

"And do not be grieved, for the joy of the LORD is your strength" (Nehemiah 8:10 ESV).

"Have you not known? Have you not heard? The everlasting God, the LORD, the Creator of the ends of the earth, neither faints nor is weary. His understanding is unsearchable. He gives power to the weak, and to those who have no might He increases strength. Even the youths shall faint and be weary, and the young men shall utterly fall, but those who wait on the LORD shall renew their strength; they shall mount up with wings like eagles, they shall run and not be weary, they shall walk and not faint" (Isaiah 40:28–31 NKJV).

"For I am honorable in the eyes of the LORD and my God has become my strength" (Isaiah 49:5 AMP).

"'For I am with you to rescue and save you,' declares the LORD. 'I will save you from the hands of the wicked and redeem you from the grasp of the cruel'" (Jeremiah 15:20–21 NIV).

"LORD, you are my strength and fortress, my refuge in the day of trouble!" (Jeremiah 16:19 NLT).

"The LORD is good, a stronghold in the day of trouble, and He knows those who take refuge in Him" (Nahum 1:7 NASB).

"Yet I will rejoice in the LORD; I will exult in the [victorious] God of my salvation! The LORD God is my Strength, my personal bravery, and my invincible army; He makes my feet like hinds' feet and will make me to walk [not to stand still in terror, but to walk] and make [spiritual] progress upon my high places [of trouble, suffering, or responsibility]!" (Habakkuk 3:18–19 AMP).

"The LORD is a refuge for the oppressed, a stronghold in times of trouble" (Psalm 9:9 NIV).

"I love you, O LORD, my strength. The LORD is my rock and my fortress and my deliverer, my God, my rock, in whom I take refuge, my shield, and the horn of my salvation, my stronghold" (Psalm 18:1–2 ESV).

"It is God who arms me with strength and makes my way perfect. He makes my feet like the feet of a deer; he enables me to stand on the heights" (Psalm 18:32–33 NIV).

"You have also given me the shield of Your salvation, and Your right hand upholds me; and Your gentleness makes me great. You enlarge my steps under me, and my feet have not slipped" (Psalm 18:35–36 NASB).

"You have set my feet in a broad place" (Psalm 31:8 AMP).

"Our soul waits for the LORD; He is our help and our shield. For our heart shall rejoice in Him, because we have trusted in His holy name. Let Your mercy, O LORD, be upon us, just as we hope in You" (Psalm 33:20–22 NKJV).

"I sought the LORD, and He answered me, and delivered me from all my fears" (Psalm 34:4 NASB).

"This poor man cried, and the LORD heard him, and saved him out of all his troubles" (Psalm 34:6 AMP).

"Yet I am poor and needy; may the LORD think of me. You are my help and my deliverer; O my God, do not delay" (Psalm 40:17 NIV).

"But why do you call Me 'Lord, Lord,' and not do the things which I say? Whoever comes to Me, and hears My sayings and does them, I will show you whom he is like: He is like a man building a house, who dug deep and laid the foundation on the rock. And when the flood arose, the stream beat vehemently against that house, and could not shake it, for it was founded on the rock. But he who heard and did nothing is like a man who built a house on the earth without a foundation, against which the stream beat vehemently; and immediately it fell. And the ruin of that house was great" (Luke 6:46–49 NKJV).

"Behold, God is my helper and ally; the LORD is my upholder and is with them who uphold my life. He will pay back evil to my enemies; in Your faithfulness [LORD] put an end to them" (Psalm 54:4–5 AMP).

"My soul, wait silently for God alone, for my expectation is from Him. He only is my rock and my salvation; He is my defense; I shall not be moved. In God is my salvation and my glory; the rock of my strength, and my refuge, is in God. Trust in Him at all times, you people; pour out your heart before Him; God is a refuge for us. Selah" (Psalm 62:5–8 NKJV).

"Be to me a rock of habitation to which I may continually come; You have given commandment to save me, for You are my rock and my fortress" (Psalm 71:3 NASB).

"For You are my hope, O LORD God; You are my trust from my youth. By You I have been upheld from birth; You are He who took me out of my mother's womb. My praise shall be continually of You. I have become as a wonder to many, but You are my strong refuge" (Psalm 71:5–7 NKJV).

"Whom have I in heaven but You? And besides You, I desire nothing on earth. My flesh and my heart may fail, but God is the strength of my heart and my portion forever" (Psalm 73:25–26 NASB).

"The horse is made ready for the day of battle, but victory rests with the LORD" (Proverbs 21:31 NIV).

"What then shall we say to these things? If God is for us, who is against us? He who did not spare His own Son, but delivered Him over for us all, how will He not also with Him freely give us all things?" (Romans 8:31–32 NASB).

"Now the body is not for sexual immorality but for the Lord, and the Lord for the body. And God both raised up the Lord and will also raise us up by His power" (1 Corinthians 6:13–14 NKJV).

"Not that we are sufficient in ourselves to claim anything as coming from us, but our sufficiency is from God" (2 Corinthians 3:5 ESV).

I can do all things through Christ who strengthens me (Philippians 4:13 NKJV).

"But the Lord is faithful, and he will strengthen and protect you from the evil one" (2 Thessalonians 3:3 NIV).

"He who dwells in the shelter of the Most High will abide in the shadow of the Almighty. I will say to the LORD, 'My refuge and my fortress, My God, in whom I trust!' For it is He who delivers you from the snare of the trapper and from the deadly pestilence. He will cover you with His pinions, and under His wings you may seek refuge; His faithfulness is a shield and bulwark" (Psalm 91:1–4 NASB).

"For He will give His angels charge concerning you, to guard you in all your ways. They will bear you up in their hands, that you do not strike your foot against a stone" (Psalm 91:11–12 NASB).

"But the LORD has become my stronghold, and my God the rock of my refuge" (Psalm 94:22 ESV).

"Then they cry to the LORD in their trouble, and He delivers them out of their distresses" (Psalm 107:19 AMP).

"Give us aid against the enemy, for the help of man is worthless. With God we will gain the victory, and he will trample down our enemies" (Psalm 108:12–13 NIV).

"Out of my distress I called on the LORD; the LORD answered me and set me free" (Psalm 118:5 ESV).

"My soul melts away for sorrow; strengthen me according to your word!" (Psalm 119:28 ESV).

"In my trouble I cried to the LORD, and He answered me. Deliver my soul, O LORD, from lying lips, from a deceitful tongue" (Psalm 120:1–2 NASB).

"I will lift up my eyes to the hills—from whence comes my help? My help comes from the LORD, who made heaven and earth. He will not allow your foot to be moved; He who keeps you will not slumber. Behold, He who keeps Israel shall neither slumber nor sleep. The LORD is your keeper" (Psalm 121:1–5 NKJV).

"Our help is in the name of the LORD, who made heaven and earth" (Psalm 124:8 NASB).

"Therefore He had to be like His brothers in every way, so that He could become a merciful and faithful high priest in service to God, to make propitiation for the sins of the people. For since He Himself was tested and has suffered, He is able to help those who are tested" (Hebrews 2:17–18 HCSB).

"For He Himself has said, 'I will never leave you nor forsake you.' So we may boldly say: 'The LORD is my helper; I will not fear. What can man do to me?'" (Hebrews 13:5–6 NKJV).

Chapter 43

PATIENCE

I am still working on this one—being patient. I feel like I am a work in progress in becoming patient, and maybe you feel the same way.

Do you get impatient waiting in line to have your groceries checked out? I used to, but now I make the waiting in line an opportunity to talk to God, plan the rest of my day, or talk to someone else waiting in line. Life is simpler and more relaxed if we decide that we are not in a hurry to get somewhere or receive something. Otherwise, our impatience can make us a nervous wreck.

If we allow ourselves to be impatient, we can cause ourselves to be anxious, frustrated, angry, unhappy, and unhealthy by increasing our blood pressure. What is the point? It accomplishes nothing good, and as we know from past experience, whatever we were so impatient about last time all worked out fine!

"Be still and rest in the LORD; wait for Him and patiently lean yourself upon Him; fret not yourself because of him who prospers in his way, because of the man who brings wicked devices to pass. Cease from anger and forsake wrath; fret not yourself—it tends only to evildoing" (Psalm 37:7–8 AMP).

"Do not be anxious about anything, but in everything, by prayer and petition, with thanksgiving, present your requests to God" (Philippians 4:6 NIV).

"Then Abraham waited patiently, and he received what God had promised" (Hebrews 6:15 NLT).

"Consider it wholly joyful, my brethren, whenever you are enveloped in or encounter trials of any sort or fall into various temptations. Be assured and understand that the trial and proving of your faith bring out endurance and steadfastness and patience. But let endurance and steadfastness and patience have full play and do a thorough work, so that you may be [people] perfectly and fully developed [with no defects], lacking in nothing" (James 1:2–4 AMP).

"Be patient, therefore, brothers, until the coming of the Lord. See how the farmer waits for the precious fruit of the earth, being patient about it, until it receives the early and the late rains. You also, be patient. Establish your hearts, for the coming of the Lord is at hand" (James 5:7–8 ESV).

"I waited patiently for the LORD; he inclined to me and heard my cry. He drew me up from the pit of destruction, out of the miry bog, and set my feet upon a rock, making my steps secure. He put a new song in my mouth, a song of praise to our God. Many will see and fear, and put their trust in the LORD" (Psalm 40:1–3 ESV).

Chapter 44

PEACE

Each one has to find his peace from within. And peace to be real
must be unaffected by outside circumstances.
—Mahatma Gandhi, Indian philosopher, internationally
esteemed for his doctrine of nonviolent protest, 1869–1948

Our daily lives seem to clothe us in noises, questions, agitations,
episodes of being hurried, and frustrations that penetrate our
whole being; there is no peace. Stop, close your eyes, and repeat the
word *peace*. You will begin to feel quietness and calmness. Your whole
body will relax.

To know God is to enshroud ourselves in a constant peace. The
only way to achieve this peace is to make room in our lives for God
by reading and meditating on His Word day and night. Through this
daily activity there will be a trust and belief in God's promises, which
will become as natural as breathing. We will experience a veil being
lifted from us as an overwhelming peace prevails, despite the turmoil
in our lives.

"The LORD replied, 'My Presence will go with you, and I will give you rest'" (Exodus 33:14 NIV).

"Those who love Your law have great peace, and nothing causes them to stumble" (Psalm 119:165 NASB).

"When a man's ways please the LORD, He makes even his enemies to be at peace with him" (Proverbs 16:7 AMP).

"You will keep him in perfect peace, whose mind is stayed on You, because he trusts in You" (Isaiah 26:3 NKJV).

"These things I have spoken to you, so that in Me you may have peace. In the world you have tribulation, but take courage; I have overcome the world" (John 16:33 NASB).

"For God is not a God of confusion but of peace" (1 Corinthians 14:33 ESV).

"And the peace of God, which transcends all understanding, will guard your hearts and your minds in Christ Jesus" (Philippians 4:7 NIV).

"And let the peace of God rule in your hearts. . . . and be thankful" (Colossians 3:15 NKJV).

"Peacemakers who sow in peace raise a harvest of righteousness" (James 3:18 NIV).

"Peace be with all of you who are in Christ" (1 Peter 5:14 NLT).

Chapter 45

PERFECT TIMING

I can't wait!" We've all said that. But waiting is easier when we know
God is making all the circumstances right, for He is giving us the
best. God's timing is perfect. Never doubt His thinking!

When I was building my house in the mountains, I thought I could
sell my house in Denver very quickly to give me the cash flow needed
for my new home. It didn't happen. My house did not sell for over a
year. My timing was not God's timing, but His timing was perfect.
With the advice of friends, I was able to get a low-interest loan to
see me through, which I believe was all orchestrated by God. When
my house sold, I was able to move my furniture and me into the new
house, so I did not need to store my furniture, spend money on a motel
room, or inconvenience a friend for living quarters.

Through other experiences too, I am now relying on God's timing
and not mine. His timing is always better!

"But as for me, my prayer is to You, O LORD, in the acceptable time"
(Psalm 69:13 NKJV).

"And God is able to make all grace abound to you, so that in all things at all times, having all that you need, you will abound in every good work" (2 Corinthians 9:8 NIV).

"So let's not get tired of doing what is good. At just the right time we will reap a harvest of blessing if we don't give up" (Galatians 6:9 NLT).

"And my God will supply every need of yours according to his riches in glory in Christ Jesus" (Philippians 4:19 ESV).

"The LORD helps the fallen and lifts those bent beneath their loads. The eyes of all look to you in hope; you give them their food as they need it. When you open your hand, you satisfy the hunger and thirst of every living thing" (Psalm 145:14–16 NLT).

Chapter 46

POVERTY

I took a one-year leave of absence from my teaching position, which meant no pay for one year, and ventured out in a selling job. I remember eating lots of peanut butter and beans that year! I was financially poor, but I still had a roof over my head, my health, friends and family who cared about me, and a teaching job to return to.

Some people who are poor do not have the luxury of returning to a job and continuing to sell part-time as I did. It is heartwarming to know that poor people throughout the world are being helped with their basic needs or trained to provide for themselves, through financial donations and volunteers.

But as this is being done, do we help the poor spiritually? This is their earthly home for a short period of time, but where will their eternal home be? Some of the poor may know God and have *true* wealth, while others are floundering day to day with little hope.

Let us not forget the less fortunate. We must do whatever we can to help the poor and pray for them that all their physical and spiritual needs are fulfilled. It will make a difference in their lives—and in ours.

"You will always have the poor among you" (Matthew 26:11 NLT).

"The wicked upset the plans of the poor, but the LORD will protect them" (Psalm 14:6 NCV).

"A poor man is better than a liar" (Proverbs 19:22 KJV).

"Better to be poor and honest than to be dishonest and rich" (Proverbs 28:6 NLT).

Chapter 47

PRAISE AND GLORY

G ive God glory and praise for everything even when you don't want to.

When I had an emergency appendectomy, a favorite verse from the Bible came to mind, since I read it almost every day: "My brethren, count it all joy when you fall into various trials" (James 1:2 NKJV). This was one of those trials, and I remember thanking Him for it. At the time of this incident, I was in North Carolina visiting a friend I had not seen for at least fifteen years. God knew that this was the right person, my angel, who got me to the right hospital. God gathered up the best doctors, nurses, a lady who addressed my spiritual needs, and a friend who gave me great comfort.

I did not question why, because I knew that God had trusted me enough to give me the opportunity to grow. God made me a true believer in His power and love for me. I praise Him and give Him the glory, for it was all for my good. The bonus that resulted was that my friend and I are closer, and I experienced the prayers of my family and friends.

No matter what the situation may be, God knows *best*. Glory and praise to God!

Praise God, from whom all blessings flow;
Praise Him, all creatures here below;
Praise Him above, ye heavenly host;
Praise Father, Son, and Holy Ghost.

—"Doxology"

"Honor the LORD for the glory of his name. Worship the LORD in the splendor of his holiness" (Psalm 29:2 NLT).

"You have turned for me my mourning into dancing; You have loosed my sackcloth and girded me with gladness, that my soul may sing praise to You and not be silent O LORD my God, I will give thanks to You forever" (Psalm 30:11–12 NASB).

"Rejoice in the LORD and be glad, you righteous; sing, all you who are upright in heart!" (Psalm 32:11 NIV).

"And one cried to another and said, Holy, holy, holy is the LORD of hosts; the whole earth is full of His glory!" (Isaiah 6:3 AMP).

"Praise the LORD in song, for He has done excellent things; let this be known throughout the earth. Cry aloud and shout for joy, O inhabitant of Zion, for great in your midst is the Holy One of Israel" (Isaiah 12:5–6 NASB).

"O LORD, You are my God; I will exalt You, I will praise Your name, for You have done wonderful things, even purposes planned of old [and fulfilled] in faithfulness and truth" (Isaiah 25:1 AMP).

"Thus says the LORD: 'Let not the wise man glory in his wisdom, let not the mighty man glory in his might, nor let the rich man glory in his riches; but let him who glories glory in this, that he understands and knows Me, that I am the LORD, exercising lovingkindness, judgment, and righteousness in the earth. For in these I delight,' says the LORD" (Jeremiah 9:23–24 NKJV).

"Heal me, O LORD, and I shall be healed; save me, and I shall be saved, for You are my praise" (Jeremiah 17:14 AMP).

"'Let the one who boasts, boast in the Lord.' For it is not the one who commends himself who is approved, but the one whom the Lord commends" (2 Corinthians 10:17–18 ESV).

"For this reason also, God highly exalted Him, and bestowed on Him the name which is above every name, so that at the name of Jesus every knee will bow, of those who are in heaven and on earth and under the earth, and that every tongue will confess that Jesus Christ is Lord, to the glory of God the Father" (Philippians 2:9–11 NASB).

"God has ascended amid shouts of joy, the LORD amid the sounding of trumpets. Sing praises to God, sing praises; sing praises to our King, sing praises. For God is the King of all the earth; sing to him a psalm of praise" (Psalm 47:5–7 NIV).

"Now all glory to God our Father forever and ever! Amen" (Philippians 4:20 NLT).

"Say to God, 'How awesome are your deeds! So great is your power that your enemies come cringing to you. All the earth worships you and sings praises to you; they sing praises to your name.' Selah" (Psalm 66:3–4 ESV).

"Let all who seek You rejoice and be glad in You; and let those who love Your salvation say continually, 'Let God be magnified'" (Psalm 70:4 NASB).

"It is good to give thanks to the LORD and to sing praises to Your name, O Most High; to declare Your lovingkindness in the morning and Your faithfulness by night" (Psalm 92:1–2 NASB).

"Oh come, let us sing to the LORD! Let us shout joyfully to the Rock of our salvation. Let us come before His presence with thanksgiving; let us shout joyfully to Him with psalms" (Psalm 95:1–2 NKJV).

"May the glory of the LORD endure forever" (Psalm 104:31 AMP).

"I will sing to the LORD as long as I live; I will sing praise to my God while I have being" (Psalm 104:33 ESV).

"Praise the LORD! I will praise the LORD with my whole heart" (Psalm 111:1 NKJV).

"From the rising of the sun to its setting, the name of the LORD is to be praised! The LORD is high above all nations, and his glory above the heavens!" (Psalm 113:3–4 ESV).

"I will give you thanks, for you answered me; you have become my salvation" (Psalm 118:21 NIV).

"You are my God, and I will praise you! You are my God, and I will exalt you!" (Psalm 118:28 NLT).

"When the righteous triumph, there is great glory" (Proverbs 28:12 ESV).

"I will extol You, my God, O King; and I will bless Your name forever and ever. Every day I will bless You, and I will praise Your name forever and ever. Great is the LORD, and greatly to be praised; and His greatness is unsearchable. One generation shall praise Your works to another, and shall declare Your mighty acts. I will meditate on the glorious splendor of Your majesty, and on Your wondrous works. Men shall speak of the might of Your awesome acts, and I will declare Your greatness. They shall utter the memory of Your great goodness, and shall sing of Your righteousness" (Psalm 145:1–7 NKJV).

"Praise the LORD! Praise the LORD, O my soul! I will praise the LORD while I live; I will sing praises to my God while I have my being" (Psalm 146:1–2 NASB).

Chapter 48

PRAYER

Can you become closer to God by talking to Him through prayer? Yes!

Prayer is a time to tell God just the way it is in your life—your gratitude, your disappointments, your problems, what you want, the needs of friends and family. Tell God everything that comes to mind. The time you take to pray will change your life, because prayer changes you. God will be your new best friend. He'll be there whenever you want to talk with Him.

But if God knows everything I am thinking, then why should I pray? Prayer is the way for us to have an intimate relationship with God. God loves to hear from us, because He wants us to experience the healing that comes from prayer, not only to us, but also to others. Prayer is letting our guard down and opening the door to unconditional love.

"And the LORD restored the fortunes of Job, when he had prayed for his friends. And the LORD gave Job twice as much as he had before" (Job 42:10 ESV).

"The LORD has heard my plea; the LORD will answer my prayer" (Psalm 6:9 NLT).

"But you, when you pray, go into your room, and when you have shut your door, pray to your Father who is in the secret place; and your Father who sees in secret will reward you openly. And when you pray, do not use vain repetitions as the heathen do. For they think that they will be heard for their many words. Therefore do not be like them. For Your Father knows the things you have need of before you ask Him. In this manner, therefore, pray:

> Our Father in heaven,
> Hallowed be Your name.
> Your kingdom come
> Your will be done
> On earth as it is in heaven.
> Give us this day our daily bread.
> And forgive us our debts,
> As we forgive our debtors.
> And do not lead us into temptation.
> But deliver us from the evil one.
> For Yours is the kingdom and the power and the glory forever.
> Amen" (Matthew 6:6–13 NKJV).

"Watch and pray so that you will not fall into temptation. The spirit is willing, but the body is weak" (Matthew 26:41 NIV).

"Is any one of you in trouble? He should pray" (James 5:13 NIV).

"Therefore, confess your sins to one another, and pray for one another so that you may be healed. The effective prayer of a righteous man can accomplish much" (James 5:16 NASB).

"Hear my prayer, O Lord; listen to my cry for mercy. In the day of my trouble I will call to you, for you will answer me" (Psalm 86:6–7 NIV).

"I love the Lord because he hears my voice and my prayer for mercy. Because he bends down to listen, I will pray as long as I have breath!" (Psalm 116:1–2 NLT).

Chapter 49

PRIDE

A proud man is always looking down on things and people; and,
of course, as long as you're looking down,
you can't see something that's above you.
—C. S. Lewis, British scholar and novelist, 1898–1963

Finding our security in God and not in man will help remove pride from our lives. We don't need to be proud as long as we have God. We don't need to prove anything to anyone, as long as we have God. God is sufficient.

It is when we forget God that we can become arrogant. We puff ourselves up with accomplishments, medals, awards, and accolades. Unfortunately, we are now focusing on man and ourselves.

Thank God when we have a success and give all the credit to Him. After all, He gave us the opportunity, the intelligence, the health, and the means to accomplish what we did. Once we realize this and focus on God, the proud feeling will never take root.

". . . because of the pride of evil men. Surely God does not hear an empty cry, nor does the Almighty regard it" (Job 35:12–13 ESV).

"The proud and haughty man—Scoffer is his name—deals and acts with overbearing pride" (Proverbs 21:24 AMP).

"You rebuke the proud—the cursed, who stray from Your commandments" (Psalm 119:21 NKJV).

"Do you see a man wise in his own eyes? There is more hope for a fool than for him" (Proverbs 26:12 NIV).

"He who is of a proud heart stirs up strife" (Proverbs 28:25 NKJV).

"Be not overly righteous, and do not make yourself too wise. Why should you destroy yourself?" (Ecclesiastes 7:16 ESV).

"Do not think of yourself more highly than you ought" (Romans 12:3 NIV).

"If anyone thinks he is something when he is nothing, he deceives himself" (Galatians 6:3 NIV).

"If anyone . . . does not consent to wholesome words, even the words of our Lord Jesus Christ, and to the doctrine which accords with godliness, he is proud, knowing nothing" (1 Timothy 6:3–4 NKJV).

Chapter 50

PROSPERITY

I t is all about God, not about us. If we can really delight ourselves in the Lord, we will prosper in life. We will find a shield around us in the most trying times. We will find the strength to forge ahead, because our focus is on God and not on ourselves. If we walk away from God, then we will find ourselves in want.

In *My Utmost for His Highest*, Oswald Chambers wrote, "'He himself shall dwell in prosperity . . .' (Psalm 25:13). God will cause us to 'dwell in prosperity,' keeping us at ease, even in the midst of tribulation, misunderstanding, and slander, if our 'life is hidden with Christ in God' (Colossians 3:3)."

"Keep the charge of the LORD your God, walking in his ways and keeping his statutes, his commandments, his rules, and his testimonies, as it is written in the Law of Moses, that you may prosper in all that you do and wherever you turn" (1 Kings 2:3 ESV).

"Only, may the LORD grant you discretion and understanding, that when he gives you charge over Israel you may keep the law of the LORD your God. Then you will prosper if you are careful to observe the statutes and the rules that the LORD commanded Moses for Israel. Be strong and courageous. Fear not; do not be dismayed" (1 Chronicles 22:12–13 ESV).

"O children of Israel, do not fight against the LORD God of your fathers, for you shall not prosper!" (2 Chronicles 13:12 NKJV).

"This is what Hezekiah did throughout Judah, doing what was good and right and faithful before the LORD his God. In everything that he undertook in the service of God's temple and in obedience to the law and the commands, he sought his God and worked wholeheartedly. And so he prospered" (2 Chronicles 31:20–21 NIV).

"The God of heaven will prosper us" (Nehemiah 2:20 AMP).

"Who are those who fear the LORD? He will show them the path they should choose. They will live in prosperity" (Psalm 25:12–13 NLT).

"But he who trusts in the LORD will prosper" (Proverbs 28:25 NASB).

Chapter 51

PROUD VS. HUMBLE

In reality there is perhaps not one of our natural passions so hard
to subdue as pride. Disguise it, struggle with it, beat it down,
stifle it, mortify it as much as one pleases, it is still alive,
and will every now and then peep out and show itself; . . .
for, even if I could conceive that I had completely overcome it,
I should probably be proud of my humility.
—Benjamin Franklin

As a teacher, I have been told in meetings that I must build up the
child's self-esteem. It sounds good and noble until you translate
the word *self-esteem*—having pride in oneself. Teachers were and are
still being told they should make the child feel prideful. Now self-
esteem doesn't sound so good.

We should want what God wants for our children. God wants us to
love ourselves, have a strong moral character, and be humble. In God's
eyes, being prideful is a sin.

Let's use God's love as an impetus to remain humble.

"When pride comes, then comes disgrace, but with the humble is wisdom" (Proverbs 11:2 ESV).

"Poverty and shame will come to him who disdains correction, but he who regards a rebuke will be honored" (Proverbs 13:18 NKJV).

"Before his downfall a man's heart is proud, but humility comes before honor" (Proverbs 18:12 NIV).

"Behold, as for the proud one, his soul is not right within him; but the righteous will live by his faith" (Habakkuk 2:4 NASB).

"That is why Scripture says: 'God opposes the proud but gives grace to the humble'" (James 4:6 NIV).

"Likewise, you who are younger, be subject to the elders. Clothe yourselves, all of you, with humility toward one another, for 'God opposes the proud but gives grace to the humble'" (1 Peter 5:5 ESV).

"A man's pride will bring him low, but he who is of a humble spirit will obtain honor" (Proverbs 29:23 AMP).

Chapter 52

REPENTANCE

Some often repent, yet never reform; they resemble a man traveling in a dangerous path, who frequently starts and stops, but never turns back.
—Bonnell Thornton

Every time we commit a particular sin, it's as if a heavy chain is being draped on our bodies, pulling us down into a dark hole. The sin comes in a variety of forms—having an unforgiving spirit, drugs, adultery, gluttony, pornography, or any bad habit. We might find pleasure in the sin, but no joy.

The numerous chains we gather as we sin are so heavy that we sink farther down in the hole, finding it harder to breathe. In desperation we reach out to God, confessing our sin and asking for His help. At that point, one chain breaks off, and it is easier to breathe. But we are still in the hole, weighed down by the other chains. Now it is imperative we change our thinking, make a plan to escape this bondage, and execute this life-saving plan every day. As we do, one by one the chains are lifted, and the hole gives way to a mountaintop. We are free and know God's joy!

This is repentance!

"Repent and turn from all your transgressions, lest iniquity be your ruin and so shall they not be a stumbling block to you. Cast away from you all your transgressions by which you have transgressed against Me, and make you a new mind and heart and a new spirit" (Ezekiel 18:30–31 AMP).

"Unless you repent, you will all likewise perish" (Luke 13:3 ESV).

"In the same way, there is more joy in heaven over one lost sinner who repents and returns to God than over ninety-nine others who are righteous and haven't strayed away!" (Luke 15:7 NLT).

"Just so, I tell you, there is joy before the angels of God over one sinner who repents" (Luke 15:10 ESV).

"Peter replied, 'Each of you must repent of your sins and turn to God, and be baptized in the name of Jesus Christ for the forgiveness of your sins. Then you will receive the gift of the Holy Spirit. This promise is to you, and to your children, and even to the Gentiles—all who have been called by the Lord our God'" (Acts 2:38–39 NLT).

"Or do you think lightly of the riches of His kindness and tolerance and patience, not knowing that the kindness of God leads you to repentance?" (Romans 2:4 NASB).

"Yet now I am happy, not because you were made sorry, but because your sorrow led you to repentance. For you became sorrowful as God intended and so were not harmed in any way by us. Godly sorrow brings repentance that leads to salvation and leaves no regret" (2 Corinthians 7:9–10 NIV).

"Put off your old self, which belongs to your former manner of life and is corrupt through deceitful desires, and . . . be renewed in the spirit of your minds, and . . . put on the new self, created after the likeness of God in true righteousness and holiness" (Ephesians 4:22–24 ESV).

"But now you yourselves are to put off all these: anger, wrath, malice, blasphemy, filthy language out of your mouth. Do not lie to one another.

. . . Put on the new man who is renewed in knowledge according to the image of Him who created him" (Colossians 3:8–10 NKJV).

"People who conceal their sins will not prosper, but if they confess and turn from them, they will receive mercy" (Proverbs 28:13 NLT).

Chapter 53

RIGHTEOUS VS. WICKED

I f you had a choice of being righteous or wicked, which would you choose? Of course, you would choose to be righteous. We all want to be righteous, but we must take a look at our actions to see if they line up with that desire.

Do we gossip about others? First Timothy 5:13 (NKJV) warns against "gossips and busybodies, saying things which they ought not."

Do we take a few office supplies home with us for our personal use? The ninth commandment says, "You shall not steal" (Exodus 20:15 NKJV).

Do we support a woman's choice to abort her baby? The American College of Pediatricians "concurs with the body of scientific evidence that human life begins at conception—fertilization."[4] There are two lives—the pregnant woman's and her unborn child's. The seventh commandment is "You shall not murder" (Exodus 20:13 NKJV).

Do we support the homosexual lifestyle? The Bible says, "If a man lies with a male as he lies with a woman, both of them have committed an abomination" (Leviticus 20:13 NKJV). "For this reason God gave them up to vile passions. For even their women exchanged the natural use for what is against nature. Likewise also the men leaving the natural use of the woman, burned in their lust for one another, men with men committing what is shameful" (Romans 1:26–27 NKJV).

Being righteous is not always the easy road to take, but we must obey God's Word. Remember the following:

1. The Bible is all true or all a lie. One cannot pick and choose what fits the way he or she wants to feel.
2. Love for a person is not a conditional entity; its quantity and degree are not to be determined by that person's beliefs or behaviors or both. You don't stop loving the person, no matter what choice he or she makes.

"The LORD preserves all who love Him, but all the wicked He will destroy" (Psalm 145:20 NKJV).

"The hope of the righteous brings joy, but the expectation of the wicked will perish. The way of the LORD is a stronghold to the blameless, but destruction to evildoers" (Proverbs 10:28–29 ESV).

"Riches do not profit in the day of wrath, but righteousness delivers from death. The righteousness of the blameless will smooth his way, but the wicked will fall by his own wickedness. The righteousness of the upright will deliver them, but the treacherous will be caught by their own greed" (Proverbs 11:4–6 NASB).

"The righteous is delivered from trouble, and the wicked walks into it instead. With his mouth the godless man would destroy his neighbor, but by knowledge the righteous are delivered. When it goes well with the righteous, the city rejoices, and when the wicked perish there are shouts of gladness" (Proverbs 11:8–10 ESV).

"The truly righteous man attains life, but he who pursues evil goes to his death" (Proverbs 11:19 NIV).

"He who earnestly seeks good finds favor, but trouble will come to him who seeks evil" (Proverbs 11:27 NKJV).

"The plans of the righteous are just, but the advice of the wicked is deceitful" (Proverbs 12:5 NIV).

"Whoever speaks the truth gives honest evidence, but a false witness utters deceit" (Proverbs 12:17 ESV).

"No ill befalls the righteous, but the wicked are filled with trouble" (Proverbs 12:21 ESV).

"The righteous should choose his friends carefully, for the way of the wicked leads them astray. In the way of righteousness is life, and in its pathway there is no death" (Proverbs 12:26, 28 NKJV).

"The life of the godly is full of light and joy, but the light of the wicked will be snuffed out" (Proverbs 13:9 NLT).

"The righteous eat to their hearts' content, but the stomach of the wicked goes hungry" (Proverbs 13:25 NIV).

"In the house of the righteous there is much treasure, but trouble befalls the income of the wicked" (Proverbs 15:6 ESV).

"The heart of the righteous ponders how to answer, but the mouth of the wicked pours out evil things" (Proverbs 15:28 ESV).

"When justice is done, it is a joy to the righteous but terror to evildoers" (Proverbs 21:15 ESV).

"Like a muddied spring or a polluted well is a righteous man who gives way to the wicked" (Proverbs 25:26 NIV).

"When the godly are in authority, the people rejoice. But when the wicked are in power, they groan" (Proverbs 29:2 NLT).

Chapter 54

RIGHTEOUSNESS

True religion is real living; living with all one's soul,
with all one's goodness and righteousness.
—Albert Einstein

In many colleges, students learn that there is no absolute truth, that whatever they want truth to be for them is truth. This attitude is a rejection of God's Word. God's laws are absolute truths. "It is impossible for God to lie" (Hebrews 6:18 NKJV). For us to live in righteousness, which comes only through Jesus, we must be as morally right as God's laws are.

Unfortunately, intellectual jargon that seems plausible distracts many students and adults, allowing them to be politically correct, not politically right. With this attitude of fitting in, they have denied themselves a righteous life filled with blessings.

"For the LORD is righteous, He loves righteousness; the upright will behold His face" (Psalm 11:7 NASB).

"The eyes of the LORD are on the righteous, and His ears are open to their cry" (Psalm 34:15 NKJV).

"The righteous cry out, and the LORD hears them; he delivers them from all their troubles" (Psalm 34:17 NIV).

"Many are the afflictions of the righteous, but the LORD delivers him out of them all" (Psalm 34:19 ESV).

"The path of the righteous is like the first gleam of dawn, shining ever brighter till the full light of day" (Proverbs 4:18 NIV).

"Those who hate the righteous will be condemned" (Psalm 34:21 ESV).

"The fruit of the righteous is a tree of life" (Proverbs 11:30 NKJV).

"Cast your burden upon the LORD and He will sustain you; He will never allow the righteous to be shaken" (Psalm 55:22 NASB).

"To do righteousness and justice is more acceptable to the LORD than sacrifice" (Proverbs 21:3 AMP).

"The [uncompromisingly] righteous shall be glad in the LORD and shall trust and take refuge in Him; and all the upright in heart shall glory and offer praise" (Psalm 64:10 AMP).

"For the LORD God is a sun and shield; the LORD will give grace and glory; no good thing will He withhold from those who walk uprightly" (Psalm 84:11 NKJV).

"Yes, the LORD will give what is good, and our land will yield its increase. Righteousness shall go before Him and shall make His footsteps a way in which to walk" (Psalm 85:12–13 AMP).

"Whoever pursues righteousness and kindness will find life, righteousness, and honor" (Proverbs 21:21 ESV).

"The righteous is concerned for the rights of the poor" (Proverbs 29:7 NASB).

"You have been set free from sin and have become slaves to righteousness" (Romans 6:18 NIV).

"The righteous shall flourish like a palm tree, he shall grow like a cedar in Lebanon. Those who are planted in the house of the LORD shall flourish in the courts of our God. They shall still bear fruit in old age; they shall be fresh and flourishing, to declare that the LORD is upright; He is my rock, and there is no unrighteousness in Him" (Psalm 92:12–15 NKJV).

"Christ is the end of the law so that there may be righteousness for everyone who believes" (Romans 10:4 NIV).

"Righteousness and justice are the foundation of His throne" (Psalm 97:2 NASB).

"Light is sown for the righteous, and joy for the upright in heart" (Psalm 97:11 ESV).

"Awake to righteousness, and do not sin; for some do not have the knowledge of God" (1 Corinthians 15:34 NKJV).

"Righteous are You, O LORD. . . . You have commanded Your testimonies in righteousness and exceeding faithfulness" (Psalm 119:137–138 NASB).

"Your righteousness is an everlasting righteousness" (Psalm 119:142 AMP).

"Your testimonies are righteous forever" (Psalm 119:144 NASB).

Chapter 55

SABBATH

The Hebrew verb *shabbath* means "to rest from labor." The seventh day of the week is the day of rest. The Jews honor this day on Saturday, and most Christians honor this day on Sunday.

When I was growing up, our family went to church and then spent time with our grandparents the rest of the day. Now it is common to find that families go to church and then come home to do work like mowing the yard.

According to the Bible, it is time to rest on the seventh day. There is no work unless it is an emergency. We need to plan our six days better to get our work done, so that we can rest on the seventh day. That may mean that we turn off the TV to get our tasks done, so that we can rest on Sunday and spend time in God's Word.

"For six days, work is to be done, but the seventh day shall be your holy day, a Sabbath of rest to the LORD" (Exodus 35:2 NIV).

"Six days shall work be done, but the seventh day is a Sabbath of solemn rest, a holy convocation. You shall do no work on it; it is the Sabbath of the LORD in all your dwellings" (Leviticus 23:3 NKJV).

"You shall keep My Sabbaths and reverence My sanctuary: I am the LORD" (Leviticus 26:2 NKJV).

"He said to them, 'Which one of you who has a sheep, if it falls into a pit on the Sabbath, will not take hold of it and lift it out? Of how much more value is a man than a sheep! So it is lawful to do good on the Sabbath'" (Matthew 12:11–12 ESV).

Chapter 56

SEEKING

I'm sure you remember the game Hide and Seek. One person counted to ten while the other children hid. When the person finished counting to ten, he would say, "Ready or not, here I come!" And away he went, seeking out his hiding friends.

It is time that we seek out God. He will thrill us as we allow Him to touch our hearts and turn our lives around. His Word will reassure us that He loves us. All we have to do is seek, and we will find joy, peace, patience, faith, endurance, love, and other good things.

Sing to Him, sing psalms to Him; talk of all His wondrous works! Glory in His holy name; let the hearts of those rejoice who seek the LORD! Seek the LORD and His strength; seek His face evermore! (1 Chronicles 16:9–11 NKJV).

"The LORD is with you when you are with Him. And if you seek Him, He will let you find Him; but if you forsake Him, He will forsake you" (2 Chronicles 15:2 NASB).

"But they who seek the LORD shall not be in want of any good thing" (Psalm 34:10 NASB).

"Turn away from evil and do good; seek peace and pursue it" (Psalm 34:14 ESV).

"You who seek God, let your hearts revive" (Psalm 69:32 ESV).

"Evil men do not understand justice, but those who seek the LORD understand it fully" (Proverbs 28:5 NIV).

"Jesus answered them and said, 'My doctrine is not Mine, but His who sent Me. If anyone wills to do His will, he shall know concerning the doctrine, whether it is from God or whether I speak on My own authority. He who speaks from himself seeks his own glory; but He who seeks the glory of the One who sent Him is true, and no unrighteousness is in Him'" (John 7:16–18 NKJV).

"Glory in His holy name; let the heart of those who seek the LORD be glad. Seek the LORD and His strength; seek His face continually. Remember His wonders which He has done, His marvels and the judgments uttered by His mouth" (Psalm 105:3–5 NASB).

Chapter 57

SHORT-LIVED

I expect to pass through this life but once. If, therefore, there be
any kindness I can show, or any good thing I can do to any fellow
being, let me do it now, and not defer or neglect it,
as I shall not pass this way again.
—William Penn

When we are young, we feel like we have forever to live on earth.
But time goes by quickly, and we do not know when God will
call us home. In the meantime, we make the most of each day on earth
by preparing ourselves physically, mentally, and spiritually, so that we
will not miss out on opportunities that come our way.

Don't chase your dreams, but reach your dreams with definite goals.
Write down your goals and act on your goals by keeping focused on
God and others as you reach them. Make a habit of asking God to
direct your paths and giving Him thanks for all He gives you.

During our time on earth, we can make a big difference in others'
lives by reaching out in prayer, with donations, and by listening to
others who need our help. Life is short. We will leave this earth with
nothing, so we should make a positive difference in our lives and in the
lives of others.

"Oh, remember that my life is a breath!" (Job 7:7 NKJV).

"Wealth can vanish in the wink of an eye. It can seem to grow wings and fly away like an eagle" (Proverbs 23:5 NCV).

"For we brought nothing into this world, and it is certain we can carry nothing out" (1 Timothy 6:7 NKJV).

"What is your life? For you are a mist that appears for a little time and then vanishes" (James 4:14 ESV).

"He remembered that they were but flesh, a wind that passes and comes not again" (Psalm 78:39 ESV).

"Man is like a breath; his days are like a passing shadow" (Psalm 144:4 ESV).

Chapter 58

SIN

To sin is a human business, to justify sins is a devilish business.
—Leo Nikolaevich Tolstoy

Sin is selfishness and rebellion against the law of God. Sin destroys. Sinful behaviors include lying, laziness, drunkenness, gluttony, vanity, pride, murder, deceit, sexual immorality, envy, and hatred. None of us is sinless, but we can improve by obeying God's commandments. Each morning when we wake up, we can ask God to help us please Him today.

To free ourselves from particular sins, we need to change. It is a known fact that change is not easy, but with God's help, it can be done. To begin, ask God to forgive you and ask for His help. It may be an easy change or a very difficult one, but don't quit, and keep your focus on God's help. The more we submit ourselves to God, the sooner we will be free from our sin. Always ask, what would Jesus do in this situation?

"O God, You know my foolishness; and my sins are not hidden from You" (Psalm 69:5 NKJV).

"Remember this, that the enemy has reproached, O LORD, and that a foolish people has blasphemed Your name" (Psalm 74:18 NKJV).

"These six things the LORD hates, yes, seven are an abomination to Him: a proud look, a lying tongue, hands that shed innocent blood, a heart that devises wicked plans, feet that are swift in running to evil, a false witness who speaks lies, and one who sows discord among brethren" (Proverbs 6:16–19 NKJV).

"Do not follow the crowd in doing wrong. When you give testimony in a lawsuit, do not pervert justice by siding with the crowd" (Exodus 23:2 NIV).

"Do not accept a bribe, for a bribe blinds those who see and twists the words of the righteous" (Exodus 23:8 NIV).

"For there is no one who does not sin" (1 Kings 8:46 NKJV).

"He who despises his neighbor sins" (Proverbs 14:21 NIV).

"Whoever mocks the poor insults his Maker; he who is glad at calamity will not go unpunished" (Proverbs 17:5 ESV).

"He who justifies the wicked and he who condemns the righteous are both alike an abomination to the LORD" (Proverbs 17:15 ESV).

"Also, to punish or fine the righteous is not good, nor to smite the noble for their uprightness" (Proverbs 17:26 AMP).

"Laziness casts one into a deep sleep, and an idle person will suffer hunger" (Proverbs 19:15 NKJV).

"Food gained by deceit is sweet to a man, but afterward his mouth will be filled with gravel" (Proverbs 20:17 AMP).

"An inheritance quickly gained at the beginning will not be blessed at the end" (Proverbs 20:21 NIV).

"Differing weights are an abomination to the LORD, and a false scale is not good" (Proverbs 20:23 NASB).

"Arrogance and pride—distinguishing marks in the wicked—are just plain sin" (Proverbs 21:4 MSG).

"Despite their desires, the lazy will come to ruin, for their hands refuse to work" (Proverbs 21:25 NLT).

"Do not look on the wine when it is red, when it sparkles in the cup, when it goes down smoothly; at the last it bites like a serpent and stings like a viper" (Proverbs 23:31–32 NASB).

"For what is the hope of the godless when God cuts him off, when God takes away his life?" (Job 27:8 ESV).

"There is not a righteous man on earth who does what is right and never sins" (Ecclesiastes 7:20 NIV).

"Do not testify against your neighbor without cause, or use your lips to deceive. Do not say, 'I'll do to him as he has done to me; I'll pay that man back for what he did'" (Proverbs 24:28–29 NIV).

"I went by the field of the lazy man, and by the vineyard of the man void of understanding; and, behold, it was all grown over with thorns, and nettles were covering its face, and its stone wall was broken down" (Proverbs 24:30–31 AMP).

"But they also have erred through wine, and through intoxicating drink are out of the way; the priest and the prophet have erred through intoxicating drink, they are swallowed up by wine, they are out of the way through intoxicating drink; they err in vision, they stumble in judgment" (Isaiah 28:7 NKJV).

"Everyone shall cast away his idols of silver and his idols of gold, which your hands have sinfully made for you" (Isaiah 31:7 ESV).

"Neither shall any strengthen himself whose life is in his iniquity" (Ezekiel 7:13 AMP).

"Like clouds and wind without rain is a man who boasts of a gift he does not give" (Proverbs 25:14 ESV).

"Like a club or a sword or a sharp arrow is the man who gives false testimony against his neighbor" (Proverbs 25:18 NIV).

"It is not good to eat much honey, nor is it glory to search out one's own glory" (Proverbs 25:27 NASB).

"A man without self-control is like a city broken into and left without walls" (Proverbs 25:28 ESV).

"The lazy man is wiser in his own eyes than seven men who can answer sensibly" (Proverbs 26:16 NKJV).

"Do not boast about tomorrow, for you do not know what a day may bring" (Proverbs 27:1 ESV).

"Jesus replied, 'I tell you the truth, everyone who sins is a slave of sin'" (John 8:34 NLT).

"But a certain man named Ananias, with Sapphira his wife, sold a possession. And he kept back part of the proceeds, his wife also being aware of it, and brought a certain part and laid it at the apostles' feet. But Peter said, 'Ananias, why has Satan filled your heart to lie to the Holy Spirit and keep back part of the price of the land for yourself? While it remained, was it not your own? And after it was sold, was it not in your own control? Why have you conceived this thing in your heart? You have not lied to men but to God'" (Acts 5:1–4 NKJV).

"Therefore do not let sin reign in your mortal body so that you obey its evil desires" (Romans 6:12 NIV).

"Flee from sexual immorality. Every other sin a person commits is outside the body, but the sexually immoral person sins against his own body" (1 Corinthians 6:18 ESV).

"The sting of death is sin" (1 Corinthians 15:56 NKJV).

"If anyone has no love for the Lord, let him be accursed. Our Lord, come!" (1 Corinthians 16:22 ESV).

"Whatever is not from faith is sin" (Romans 14:23 NASB).

"But now that you have come to know God, or rather to be known by God, how is it that you turn back again to the weak and worthless elemental things, to which you desire to be enslaved all over again?" (Galatians 4:9 NASB).

"Now the works of the flesh are evident, which are: adultery, fornication, uncleanness, lewdness, idolatry, sorcery, hatred, contentions, jealousies, outbursts of wrath, selfish ambitions, dissensions, heresies, envy, murders, drunkenness, revelries, and the like; of which I tell you beforehand, just as I also told you in time past, that those who practice such things will not inherit the kingdom of God" (Galatians 5:19–21 NKJV).

"For God did not call us to be impure, but to live a holy life. Therefore, he who rejects this instruction does not reject man but God, who gives you his Holy Spirit" (1 Thessalonians 4:7–8 NIV).

"Take care, brothers, lest there be in any of you an evil, unbelieving heart, leading you to fall away from the living God. But exhort one another every day, as long as it is called 'today,' that none of you may be hardened by the deceitfulness of sin" (Hebrews 3:12–13 ESV).

"Let no one say when he is tempted, 'I am being tempted by God'; for God cannot be tempted by evil, and He Himself does not tempt anyone. But each one is tempted when he is carried away and enticed by his own lust. Then when lust has conceived, it gives birth to sin; and when sin is accomplished, it brings forth death" (James 1:13–15 NASB).

"But don't just listen to God's word. You must do what it says. Otherwise, you are only fooling yourselves" (James 1:22 NLT).

"So whoever knows the right thing to do and fails to do it, for him it is sin" (James 4:17 ESV).

"A man who flatters his neighbor spreads a net for his own feet" (Proverbs 29:5 AMP).

"Do not grumble against one another, brothers, so that you may not be judged" (James 5:9 ESV).

"They promise freedom, but they themselves are slaves of sin and corruption. For you are a slave to whatever controls you" (2 Peter 2:19 NLT).

"If we say we have no sin, we deceive ourselves, and the truth is not in us" (1 John 1:8 ESV).

Chapter 59

SOWING AND REAPING

Good thoughts bear good fruit, bad thoughts bear bad fruit.
—James Lane Allen

A little child can learn the concept of sowing and reaping by taking a seed, planting it, watering it, tending it, and getting the results of a plant bearing fruit to eat. This is an analogy that children can understand. The child realizes that he will not have fruit unless he begins by planting the seed and nurturing it.

It is a simple theory, so why don't we pay closer attention to it in our daily lives? When someone needs help, do we respond that we are too busy? If someone speaks rudely to us, do we respond in the same manner, or do we take the high road by responding in a Christlike way? The Golden Rule comes to mind: Do unto others as you would have them do unto you.

Whatever you do, consider the future consequences. Your action will come back to you. Maybe not immediately, but it will.

"Tell the righteous it will be well with them, for they will enjoy the fruit of their deeds" (Isaiah 3:10 NIV).

"The heart is deceitful above all things, and desperately sick; who can understand it? 'I the LORD search the heart and test the mind, to give every man according to his ways, according to the fruit of his deeds'" (Jeremiah 17:9–10 ESV).

"Now the end has come upon you, and I will send My anger against you; I will judge you according to your ways, and I will repay you for all your abominations. My eye will not spare you, nor will I have pity; but I will repay your ways, and your abominations will be in your midst; then you shall know that I am the LORD!" (Ezekiel 7:3–4 NKJV).

"Do to others as you would have them do to you" (Luke 6:31 NIV).

"Give, and it will be given to you. Good measure, pressed down, shaken together, running over, will be put into your lap. For with the measure you use it will be measured back to you" (Luke 6:38 ESV).

"The point is this: whoever sows sparingly will also reap sparingly, and whoever sows bountifully will also reap bountifully" (2 Corinthians 9:6 ESV).

"The one who sows to please his sinful nature, from that nature will reap destruction; the one who sows to please the Spirit, from the Spirit will reap eternal life" (Galatians 6:8 NIV).

"A generous man will prosper; he who refreshes others will himself be refreshed" (Proverbs 11:25 NIV).

"Whoever sows injustice will reap calamity, and the rod of his fury will fail" (Proverbs 22:8 ESV).

"Whoever oppresses the poor to increase his own wealth, or gives to the rich, will only come to poverty" (Proverbs 22:16 ESV).

"Do not exploit the poor because they are poor and do not crush the needy in court, for the LORD will take up their case and will plunder those who plunder them" (Proverbs 22:22–23 NIV).

"For you yourselves know how you ought to follow us, for we were not disorderly among you; nor did we eat anyone's bread free of charge, but worked with labor and toil night and day, that we might not be a burden to any of you, not because we do not have authority, but to make ourselves an example of how you should follow us. For even when we were with you, we commanded you this: If anyone will not work, neither shall he eat" (2 Thessalonians 3:7–10 NKJV).

"Whoever works his land will have plenty of bread, but he who follows worthless pursuits will have plenty of poverty" (Proverbs 28:19 ESV).

Chapter 60

THANKFULNESS

A thankful spirit will reap many rewards.

How often during the day do you say "Thank you, God"? Once? two–four times? five–ten times? Never?

How often during the day *should* you say "Thank you, God"? Once? two–four times? five–ten times? Never?

Make it a habit to give God thanks. Thank Him for the clean water you drink. Thank Him when you remember someone's birthday. Thank Him for the good night's sleep you finally got. Thank Him for the illness. Wait a minute!—thank God for my disease? Yes.

God allows difficult times such as illnesses in our lives, because He knows that we can handle them with His help. He also knows that this is a great opportunity for us to grow. We may find growth in patience, persistence, faith, wisdom, courage, or some combination of these traits. Be assured that God's plans are the best, so give thanks even though you don't see beyond the immediate circumstances.

Being thankful to God in our joys and our trials will draw Him closer to us.

"Giving thanks always for all things to God the Father in the name of our Lord Jesus Christ" (Ephesians 5:20 NKJV).

"Be thankful to Him, and bless His name" (Psalm 100:4 NKJV).

"Oh, give thanks to the LORD, for He is good! For His mercy endures forever" (Psalm 106:1 NKJV). Note: Psalm 118:1 and 29 are the same as this passage.

"Let them thank the LORD for his steadfast love, for his wondrous works to the children of man! For he satisfies the longing soul, and the hungry soul he fills with good things" (Psalm 107:8–9 ESV).

"Let the word of Christ richly dwell within you, with all wisdom teaching and admonishing one another with psalms and hymns and spiritual songs, singing with thankfulness in your hearts to God. Whatever you do in word or deed, do all in the name of the Lord Jesus, giving thanks through Him to God the Father" (Colossians 3:16–17 NASB).

"For this reason we also thank God without ceasing, because when you received the word of God which you heard from us, you welcomed it not as the word of men, but as it is in truth, the word of God, which also effectively works in you who believe" (1 Thessalonians 2:13 NKJV).

Chapter 61

TITHES AND
OFFERINGS

J. C. Penny created the department store. H. J. Heinz is famous for his ketchup. Henry Crowell began Quaker Oats. Stanley Tam is the founder of the United States Plastic Corporation. These are just a few men who gave at least ten percent of their income—a *tithe*—to God because they believed God's promise about tithing: "Bring all the tithes into the storehouse . . . and prove Me now in this . . . if I will not open for you the windows of heaven and pour out for you such blessing that there will not be room enough to receive it" (Malachi 3:10 KJV).[5] Through their tithing, these men were blessed abundantly.

All that we have is God-given. God is asking only that we give ten percent of our earnings back to Him. If we honor our heavenly Father and give joyously, He will keep His promise to prosper us. We cannot outgive God.

"Every man shall give as he is able, according to the blessing of the LORD your God which He has given you" (Deuteronomy 16:17 AMP).

"Honor the LORD with your possessions, and with the firstfruits of all your increase; so your barns will be filled with plenty, and your vats will overflow with new wine" (Proverbs 3:9–10 NKJV).

"Will a man rob God? Yet you are robbing Me! But you say, 'How have we robbed You?' In tithes and offerings" (Malachi 3:8 NASB).

"Do not lay up for yourselves treasures on earth, where moth and rust destroy and where thieves break in and steal, but lay up for yourselves treasures in heaven, where neither moth nor rust destroys and where thieves do not break in and steal" (Matthew 6:19–20 ESV).

"Calling His disciples to Him, He said to them, 'Truly I say to you, this poor widow put in more than all the contributors to the treasury; for they all put in out of their surplus, but she, out of her poverty, put in all she owned, all she had to live on'" (Mark 12:43–44 NASB).

"Zaccheus stopped and said to the Lord, 'Behold, Lord, half of my possessions I will give to the poor, and if I have defrauded anyone of anything, I will give back four times as much.' And Jesus said to him, 'Today salvation has come to this house'" (Luke 19:8–9 NASB).

"Now I will write about the collection of money for God's people. Do the same thing I told the Galatian churches to do: On the first day of every week, each one of you should put aside money as you have been blessed" (1 Corinthians 16:1–2 NCV).

Chapter 62

TRUST IN GOD

You are involved in a family crisis or are in a serious automobile accident. Wrapped up in the moment, you may lose sight of God and let your emotions take over. You will be anxiety-driven instead of God-driven. Anxiety-driven is a malaise of thoughts completely out of control, while God-driven is clear thinking with quietness amid all the confusion.

Many stories from the Bible (I mention a few at the end of this book) reveal how people trusted God with an unshakable faith. Many present-day stories can also encourage you to trust God. You can find some of them in *Guideposts* magazine.

No matter how bad the situation looks to us, God sees it totally differently. He wants us to trust Him, so we can come through it gloriously. "Trust in the LORD with all your heart, and lean not on your own understanding" (Proverbs 3:5 NKJV).

"And put your trust in the LORD" (Psalm 4:5 NKJV).

"O LORD my God, in You I put my trust; save me from all those who persecute me; and deliver me" (Psalm 7:1 NKJV).

"And those who know Your name will put their trust in You, for You, O LORD, have not forsaken those who seek You" (Psalm 9:10 NASB).

"In the LORD I put my trust" (Psalm 11:1 NKJV).

"But I have trusted in Your lovingkindness; my heart shall rejoice in Your salvation. I will sing to the LORD, because He has dealt bountifully with me" (Psalm 13:5–6 NASB).

"Preserve me, O God, for in You I put my trust" (Psalm 16:1 NKJV).

"Trust in the LORD with all your heart and do not lean on your own understanding. In all your ways acknowledge Him, and He will make your paths straight" (Proverbs 3:5–6 NASB).

"As for God, His way is perfect; the word of the LORD is proven; He is a shield to all who trust in Him" (Psalm 18:30 NKJV). Note: Second Samuel 22:31 is the same as this passage.

"In You our fathers trusted; they trusted and You delivered them" (Psalm 22:4 NASB).

"To You, O LORD, I lift up my soul. O my God, I trust in You" (Psalm 25:1–2 NKJV).

"O keep me, LORD, and deliver me; let me not be ashamed or disappointed, for my trust and my refuge are in You" (Psalm 25:20 AMP).

"Blessed be the LORD, because He has heard the voice of my supplications! The LORD is my strength and my shield; my heart trusted in Him, and I am helped" (Psalm 28:6–7 NKJV).

"Incline your ear, and hear the words of the wise, and apply your heart to my knowledge, for it will be pleasant if you keep them within you, if all of them are ready on your lips. That your trust may be in the LORD, I have made them known to you today, even to you" (Proverbs 22:17–19 ESV).

"Fear of man will prove to be a snare, but whoever trusts in the LORD is kept safe" (Proverbs 29:25 NIV).

"Every word of God is pure; He is a shield to those who put their trust in Him" (Proverbs 30:5 NKJV).

"In you, O LORD, do I put my trust and seek refuge" (Psalm 31:1 AMP).

"I hate those who pay regard to worthless idols, but I trust in the LORD" (Psalm 31:6 ESV).

"But as for me, I trust in You, O LORD; I say, 'You are my God'" (Psalm 31:14 NKJV).

"How great is Your goodness, which You have stored up for those who fear You, which You have wrought for those who take refuge in You, before the sons of men!" (Psalm 31:19 NASB).

"Many are the woes of the wicked, but the LORD's unfailing love surrounds the man who trusts in him" (Psalm 32:10 NIV).

"Oh, taste and see that the LORD is good; blessed is the man who trusts in Him!" (Psalm 34:8 NKJV).

"Trust in the LORD, and do good; dwell in the land, and feed on His faithfulness" (Psalm 37:3 NKJV).

"But the salvation of the righteous is from the LORD; He is their strength in the time of trouble. And the LORD shall help them and deliver them; He shall deliver them from the wicked, and save them, because they trust in Him" (Psalm 37:39–40 NKJV).

"And he said, 'Naked I came from my mother's womb, and naked shall I return. The LORD gave, and the LORD has taken away; blessed be the name of the LORD.' In all this Job did not sin or charge God with wrong" (Job 1:21–22 ESV).

"Shall we indeed accept good from God, and shall we not accept adversity?" (Job 2:10 NKJV).

"Though He slay me, yet will I trust Him" (Job 13:15 NKJV).

"Who among you fears the LORD and obeys his servant? If you are walking in darkness, without a ray of light, trust in the LORD and rely on your God" (Isaiah 50:10 NLT).

"I will save you; you will not fall by the sword but will escape with your life, because you trust in me, declares the LORD" (Jeremiah 39:18 NIV).

"When I am afraid, I will put my trust in You. In God, whose word I praise, in God I have put my trust; I shall not be afraid. What can mere man do to me?" (Psalm 56:3–4 NASB).

"When I cry out to You, then my enemies will turn back; this I know, because God is for me. In God (I will praise His word), in the LORD (I will praise His word), in God I have put my trust; I will not be afraid. What can man do to me?" (Psalm 56:9–11 NKJV).

"And in His name Gentiles will trust" (Matthew 12:21 NKJV).

"Indeed, we had the sentence of death within ourselves so that we would not trust in ourselves, but in God who raises the dead; who delivered us from so great a peril of death, and will deliver us, He on whom we have set our hope. And He will yet deliver us" (2 Corinthians 1:9–10 NASB).

"For You have been a shelter and a refuge for me, a strong tower against the adversary. I will dwell in Your tabernacle forever; let me find refuge and trust in the shelter of Your wings. Selah [pause, and calmly think of that]!" (Psalm 61:3–4 AMP).

"O LORD of hosts, how blessed is the man who trusts in You!" (Psalm 84:12 NASB).

"Now she who is really a widow, and left alone, trusts in God and continues in supplications and prayers night and day" (1 Timothy 5:5 NKJV).

"Teach those who are rich in this world not to be proud and not to trust in their money, which is so unreliable. Their trust should be in God, who richly gives us all we need for our enjoyment. Tell them to use their money to do good. They should be rich in good works and generous to those in need, always being ready to share with others" (1 Timothy 6:17–18 NLT).

"It is better to take refuge in the LORD than to trust in man" (Psalm 118:8 ESV).

Chapter 63

TRUTH

The truth will set you free. At times, we know the truth will hurt others, but it is still the truth and needs to be told.

I remember an episode of *The Andy Griffith Show* in which the schoolchildren had to write about the Battle of Mayberry for the town newspaper. The best-written paper on the subject would appear on the front page. Of course, everyone in the town thought that his or her ancestor played the most significant role in this battle. Opie became confused because everybody's story was so different. Opie went to Mount Pilot's library to research the battle and found the facts to be opposite of what the folks in Mayberry believed.

Opie's paper appeared on the front page of the newspaper, because it was accurate and the best written. Andy was hoping that Opie's paper would not win, because it would shatter the beliefs of so many people; the truth would be hard to swallow. And it was. For over a week, the townspeople reacted unfavorably to Opie and his family until the governor, in a radio broadcast, congratulated Opie for having the courage to tell the truth and complimented the people of Mayberry on their wonderful town.

There is always freedom in the truth.

"Teach me Your way, O Lord; I will walk in Your truth; unite my heart to fear Your name" (Psalm 86:11 NASB).

"His faithfulness and truth endure to all generations" (Psalm 100:5 AMP).

"The works of His hands are truth and justice; all His precepts are sure. They are upheld forever and ever; they are performed in truth and uprightness" (Psalm 111:7–8 NASB).

"For His mercy and loving-kindness are great toward us, and the truth and faithfulness of the Lord endure forever. Praise the Lord! (Hallelujah!)" (Psalm 117:2 AMP).

"Then Jesus said to those Jews who believed Him, 'If you abide in My word, you are My disciples indeed. And you shall know the truth, and the truth shall make you free'" (John 8:31–32 NKJV).

"Your word is truth" (John 17:17 NASB). Note: Jesus is speaking about God.

"Jesus answered, 'You say rightly that I am a king. For this cause I was born, and for this cause I have come into the world, that I should bear witness to the truth. Everyone who is of the truth hears My voice'" (John 18:37 NKJV).

"We may lead a quiet and peaceable life in all godliness and reverence. For this is good and acceptable in the sight of God our Savior, who desires all men to be saved and to come to the knowledge of the truth. For there is one God and one Mediator between God and men, the Man Christ Jesus, who gave Himself a ransom for all" (1 Timothy 2:2–6 NKJV).

"And Your law is truth" (Psalm 119:142 AMP).

"You are near, O Lord, and all Your commandments are truth" (Psalm 119:151 NASB).

"The sum of Your word is truth" (Psalm 119:160 AMP).

"Little children, let us not love in word or talk but in deed and in truth" (1 John 3:18 ESV).

Chapter 64

WAY OF GOD

Reading God's mind by reading the Bible will give you a closer look at who your heavenly Father is, what He expects from you, and what you can expect in return from Him. There is nothing more valuable than the love God has for each of us. God may have to discipline us for our wrong actions, but that is the way we learn. When we fall, He is there to help us up.

God loves you unconditionally. He will do whatever He can to make your life better, but you will have to ask Him to come into your life.

"The LORD is slow to anger and abounding in steadfast love, forgiving iniquity and transgression" (Numbers 14:18 ESV).

"For the Amalekites and the Canaanites are there before you, and you shall fall by the sword; because you have turned away from the LORD, the LORD will not be with you" (Numbers 14:43 NKJV).

"But from there you will seek the LORD your God, and you will find Him if you search for Him with all your heart and all your soul. When you are in distress and all these things have come upon you, in the latter days you will return to the LORD your God and listen to His voice. For the LORD your God is a compassionate God; He will not fail you nor destroy you nor forget the covenant with your fathers which He swore to them" (Deuteronomy 4:29–31 NASB).

"He is the Rock, His work is perfect, for all His ways are law and justice. A God of faithfulness without breach or deviation, just and right is He" (Deuteronomy 32:4 AMP).

"O LORD our God, all this abundance that we have provided to build You a house for Your holy name, it is from Your hand, and all is Yours" (1 Chronicles 29:16 NASB).

"In a dream, in a vision of the night, when deep sleep falls upon men, while slumbering on their beds, then He opens the ears of men, and seals their instruction" (Job 33:15–16 NKJV).

"Lift up the light of Your countenance upon us, O LORD! You have put gladness in my heart, more than when their grain and new wine abound. In peace I will both lie down and sleep, for You alone, O LORD, make me to dwell in safety" (Psalm 4:6–8 NASB).

"For You are not a God who takes pleasure in wickedness, nor shall evil dwell with You. The boastful shall not stand in Your sight; You hate all workers of iniquity" (Psalm 5:4–5 NKJV).

"As he came from his mother's womb he shall go again, naked as he came, and shall take nothing for his toil that he may carry away in his hand" (Ecclesiastes 5:15 ESV).

"That the righteous and the wise and what they do are in God's hands, but no man knows whether love or hate awaits him. All share a common destiny—the righteous and the wicked, the good and the bad, the clean and the unclean, those who offer sacrifices and those who do not. As it is with the good man, so with the sinner; as it is with those who take oaths, so with those who are afraid to take them" (Ecclesiastes 9:1–2 NIV).

"I, the LORD, speak the truth; I declare what is right" (Isaiah 45:19 NIV).

"I will cleanse them from all their iniquity by which they have sinned against Me, and I will pardon all their iniquities by which they have sinned and by which they have transgressed against Me. Then it shall be to Me a name of joy, a praise, and an honor before all nations of the earth, who shall hear all the good that I do to them; they shall fear and tremble for all the goodness and all the prosperity that I provide for it" (Jeremiah 33:8–9 NKJV).

"You shall know that I have not done without cause all that I have done in it, declares the LORD GOD" (Ezekiel 14:23 ESV).

"Yet the children of your people say, 'The way of the LORD is not fair.' But it is their way which is not fair!" (Ezekiel 33:17 NKJV).

"Daniel answered, Blessed be the name of God forever and ever! For wisdom and might are His! He changes the times and the seasons; He removes kings and sets up kings. He gives wisdom to the wise and knowledge to those who have understanding! He reveals the deep and secret things; He knows what is in the darkness, and the light dwells with Him!" (Daniel 2:20–22 AMP).

"For I know that You are a gracious and merciful God, slow to anger and abundant in lovingkindness, One who relents from doing harm" (Jonah 4:2 NKJV).

"I will instruct you and teach you in the way you should go; I will guide you with My eye" (Psalm 32:8 NKJV).

"For the word of the LORD is right, and all His work is done in truth. He loves righteousness and justice; the earth is full of the goodness of the LORD" (Psalm 33:4–5 NKJV).

"Bless our God, O peoples, give Him grateful thanks and make the voice of His praise be heard, who put and kept us among the living, and has not allowed our feet to slip. For You, O God, have proved us; You have tried us as silver is tried, refined, and purified" (Psalm 66:8–10 AMP).

"His name shall endure forever; His name shall continue as long as the sun. And men shall be blessed in Him; all nations shall call Him blessed. Blessed be the LORD God, the God of Israel, who only does wondrous things! And blessed be His glorious name forever! And let the whole earth be filled with His glory. Amen and Amen" (Psalm 72:17–19 NKJV).

"For nothing is impossible with God" (Luke 1:37 NIV).

"As it is written in the book of the words of Isaiah the prophet, saying: 'The voice of one crying in the wilderness: "Prepare the way of the LORD; make His paths straight. Every valley shall be filled and every mountain and hill brought low; the crooked places shall be made straight and the rough ways smooth; and all flesh shall see the salvation of God"'" (Luke 3:4–6 NKJV).

"And all were astonished at the majesty of God" (Luke 9:43 ESV).

"He who believes in Him is not judged; he who does not believe has been judged already, because he has not believed in the name of the only begotten Son of God" (John 3:18 NASB).

"The mind of man plans his way, but the LORD directs his steps" (Proverbs 16:9 NASB).

"A man's steps are directed by the LORD. How then can anyone understand his own way?" (Proverbs 20:24 NIV).

"But you, O LORD, are a God merciful and gracious, slow to anger and abounding in steadfast love and faithfulness" (Psalm 86:15 ESV).

"Righteousness and justice are the foundation of Your throne" (Psalm 89:14 AMP).

"Whoever slanders his neighbor secretly I will destroy. Whoever has a haughty look and an arrogant heart I will not endure" (Psalm 101:5 ESV).

"For the wrath of God is revealed from heaven against all ungodliness and unrighteousness of men, who by their unrighteousness suppress the truth. For what can be known about God is plain to them, because God has shown it to them" (Romans 1:18–19 ESV).

"'Vengeance is Mine, I will repay,' says the Lord. Therefore 'If your enemy is hungry, feed him; if he is thirsty, give him a drink'" (Romans 12:19–20 NKJV).

"For by grace you have been saved through faith. And this is not your own doing; it is the gift of God, not a result of works" (Ephesians 2:8–9 ESV).

"For of this you can be sure: No immoral, impure or greedy person—such a man is an idolater—has any inheritance in the kingdom of Christ and of God. Let no one deceive you with empty words, for because of such things God's wrath comes on those who are disobedient" (Ephesians 5:5–6 NIV).

"For God gave us a spirit not of fear but of power and love and self-control" (2 Timothy 1:7 ESV).

"All Scripture is given by inspiration of God" (2 Timothy 3:16 NKJV).

"It is impossible for God to lie" (Hebrews 6:18 NLT).

"All flesh is as grass, and all the glory of man as the flower of the grass. The grass withers, and its flower falls away, but the word of the LORD endures forever" (1 Peter 1:24–25 NKJV).

"Grace and peace be multiplied to you in the knowledge of God and of Jesus our Lord, as His divine power has given to us all things that pertain to life and godliness, through the knowledge of Him who called us by glory and virtue, by which have been given to us exceedingly great and precious promises, that through these you may be partakers of the divine nature, having escaped the corruption that is in the world through lust" (2 Peter 1:2–4 NKJV).

"Nevertheless, do not let this one fact escape you, beloved, that with the Lord one day is as a thousand years and a thousand years as one day" (2 Peter 3:8 AMP).

"The Lord is not slow about His promise, as some count slowness, but is patient toward you, not wishing for any to perish but for all to come to repentance" (2 Peter 3:9 NASB).

"God is light and in Him is no darkness at all. If we say that we have fellowship with Him, and walk in darkness, we lie and do not practice the truth. But if we walk in the light as He is in the light, we have fellowship with one another, and the blood of Jesus Christ His Son cleanses us from all sin" (1 John 1:5–7 NKJV).

"By this the love of God was manifested in us, that God has sent His only begotten Son into the world so that we might live through Him.

In this is love, not that we loved God, but that He loved us and sent His Son to be the propitiation for our sins" (1 John 4:9–10 NASB).

"The LORD is gracious and merciful; slow to anger and great in loving-kindness. The LORD is good to all, and His mercies are over all His works" (Psalm 145:8–9 NASB).

"The LORD is righteous in all His ways, gracious in all His works. The LORD is near to all who call upon Him, to all who call upon Him in truth. He will fulfill the desire of those who fear Him; He also will hear their cry and save them" (Psalm 145:17–19 NKJV).

"Happy is he . . . whose hope is in the LORD his God, who made heaven and earth, the sea, and all that is in them; who keeps truth forever, who executes justice for the oppressed, who gives food to the hungry. The LORD gives freedom to the prisoners. The LORD opens the eyes of the blind; the LORD raises those who are bowed down; the LORD loves the righteous. The LORD watches over the strangers; He relieves the fatherless and widow; but the way of the wicked He turns upside down" (Psalm 146:5–9 NKJV).

Chapter 65

WICKED VS. RIGHTEOUS

Are you prepared when, unexpectedly, your boss confronts you with an unscrupulous plan that will promote and financially benefit the company and you? This means you can help your family financially, give more money to worthy causes and the church, and benefit the company at the same time. Do you go along with this?

Before you answer, there are more circumstances to consider. You are having financial problems because of an ongoing medical problem. This unscrupulous plan will not be known by anyone.

Now you probably feel like the man in the cartoon who has the devil on one side saying, "Go on, think of your family," and the angel on the other side saying, "No! God is your source." What will be your decision? What would God's decision be? Who knows best, you or God?

If we brand our hearts with absolute morals, we will find a way to walk the path of truth, "that the LORD your God may show us the way in which we should walk and the thing we should do" (Jeremiah 42:3 NKJV).

"But if a wicked man turns from all his sins which he has committed, keeps all My statutes, and does what is lawful and right, he shall surely live; he shall not die. None of the transgressions which he has committed shall be remembered against him; because of the righteousness which he has done, he shall live" (Ezekiel 18:21–22 NKJV).

"Better the little that the righteous have than the wealth of many wicked; for the power of the wicked will be broken, but the LORD upholds the righteous" (Psalm 37:16–17 NIV).

"The LORD's curse is on the house of the wicked, but he blesses the home of the righteous" (Proverbs 3:33 NIV).

"Whoever trusts in his riches will fall, but the righteous will flourish like a green leaf" (Proverbs 11:28 ESV).

"A man cannot be established through wickedness, but the righteous cannot be uprooted" (Proverbs 12:3 NIV).

"The wicked are overthrown and are no more, but the house of the righteous will stand" (Proverbs 12:7 NKJV).

"Whoever is wicked covets the spoil of evildoers, but the root of the righteous bears fruit. An evil man is ensnared by the transgression of his lips, but the righteous escapes from trouble" (Proverbs 12:12–13 ESV).

"Wealth gained by dishonesty will be diminished, but he who gathers by labor will increase" (Proverbs 13:11 NKJV).

"The faithless will be fully repaid for their ways, and the good man rewarded for his" (Proverbs 14:14 NIV).

"When calamity comes, the wicked are brought down, but even in death the righteous have a refuge" (Proverbs 14:32 NIV).

"A hot-tempered man stirs up strife, but the slow to anger calms a dispute. The way of the lazy is as a hedge of thorns, but the path of the upright is a highway" (Proverbs 15:18–19 NASB).

"For as by one man's disobedience many were made sinners, so also by one Man's obedience many will be made righteous" (Romans 5:19 NKJV). Note: *One man's disobedience* refers to Adam and *one Man's obedience* refers to Jesus.

"Whoever is greedy for unjust gain troubles his own household, but he who hates bribes will live. The LORD is far from the wicked, but he hears the prayer of the righteous" (Proverbs 15:27, 29 ESV).

"The highway of the upright avoids evil; he who guards his way guards his life" (Proverbs 16:17 NIV).

"All day long they wish for more, but good people give without holding back" (Proverbs 21:26 NCV).

"The wicked flee when no one pursues, but the righteous are bold as a lion" (Proverbs 28:1 ESV).

"When the wicked rise, people hide themselves, but when they perish, the righteous increase" (Proverbs 28:28 ESV).

Chapter 66

WICKEDNESS

Wickedness is weakness.
—John Milton

The foolish and wicked practice of profane cursing and
swearing is a vice so mean and low that every person
of sense and character detests and despises it.
—George Washington

Wicked men obey out of fear; good men, out of love.
—Aristotle

Every day we are bombarded with wickedness as we watch movies,
sitcoms, soap operas, local and national news, and view content
on the Internet. Evil behavior, talk, and thinking are rampant in
schools, work environments, and social activities. Violent computer
and video games entice young people. Wickedness is all around us.
Some is easy to see, and we can avoid it. But be alert to avoid being
drawn into wickedness just because others do it or because some evil
schemes are promoted by people dressed up in pretty suits and smiles.
Drape yourself in righteousness to protect yourself from wickedness.

God's Word will help you avoid the traps of wickedness. The more you know the Bible, the better equipped you will be to discern good from evil and to make wise choices to avoid its traps.

"I have seen a wicked and ruthless man flourishing like a green tree in its native soil, but he soon passed away and was no more" (Psalm 37:35–36 NIV).

"For the devious person is an abomination to the LORD" (Proverbs 3:32 ESV).

"The wicked accepts a bribe in secret to pervert the ways of justice" (Proverbs 17:23 ESV).

"The violence of the wicked sweeps them away, because they refuse to do what is just" (Proverbs 21:7 NLT).

"The soul of the wicked desires evil; his neighbor finds no favor in his eyes" (Proverbs 21:10 NASB).

"The righteous God wisely considers the house of the wicked, overthrowing the wicked for their wickedness" (Proverbs 21:12 NKJV).

"Whoever stops his ears at the cry of the poor will cry out himself and not be heard" (Proverbs 21:13 AMP).

"The sacrifice of the wicked is detestable—how much more so when brought with evil intent!" (Proverbs 21:27 NIV).

"Unless you have the extra cash on hand, don't countersign a note. Why risk everything you own? They'll even take your bed!" (Proverbs 22:26–27 TLB).

"Just as damaging as a madman shooting a deadly weapon is someone who lies to a friend and then says, 'I was only joking'" (Proverbs 26:18–19 NLT).

"His speech is smooth as butter, yet war is in his heart; his words are more soothing than oil, yet they are drawn swords" (Psalm 55:21 NIV).

"As the proverb of the ancients says, 'Wickedness proceeds from the wicked'" (1 Samuel 24:13 NKJV).

"But You, O LORD, are on high forever. For, behold, Your enemies, O LORD, for, behold, Your enemies will perish; all who do iniquity will be scattered" (Psalm 92:8–9 NASB).

"Be not overly wicked, neither be a fool. Why should you die before your time?" (Ecclesiastes 7:17 ESV).

"You felt secure in your wickedness, you said, 'No one sees me'; your wisdom and your knowledge led you astray, and you said in your heart, 'I am, and there is no one besides me.' But evil shall come upon you, which you will not know how to charm away; disaster shall fall upon you, for which you will not be able to atone; and ruin shall come upon you suddenly, of which you know nothing" (Isaiah 47:10–11 ESV).

"'There is no peace,' says the LORD, 'for the wicked'" (Isaiah 48:22 NKJV).

"But the wicked are like the troubled sea, when it cannot rest, whose waters cast up mire and dirt. 'There is no peace,' says my God, 'for the wicked'" (Isaiah 57:20–21 NKJV).

"Whoever hates disguises himself with his lips and harbors deceit in his heart; when he speaks graciously, believe him not, for there are seven abominations in his heart; though his hatred be covered with deception, his wickedness will be exposed in the assembly" (Proverbs 26:24–26 ESV).

"Salvation is far from the wicked, for they seek not nor hunger for Your statutes" (Psalm 119:155 AMP).

"Like a roaring lion or a charging bear is a wicked man ruling over a helpless people" (Proverbs 28:15 NIV).

"And if I say to the wicked man, 'You will surely die,' but he then turns away from his sin and does what is just and right—if he gives back what he took in pledge for a loan, returns what he has stolen, follows the decrees that give life, and does no evil, he will surely live; he will not die. None of the sins he has committed will be remembered against him. He has done what is just and right; he will surely live" (Ezekiel 33:14–16 NIV).

Chapter 67

WISDOM

He has power reflecting from his eyes because he is so wise.
—Rita Hannele Hawi, "Old Wise Man"

Some people confuse intelligence with wisdom. Being intelligent, according to the dictionary, is showing sound judgment and rationality, being mentally acute, and having a capacity to acquire and apply knowledge. Wisdom is far more encompassing. Wisdom knows what is true, right, or lasting. Having understanding and discernment will help you gain wisdom, but only when you ask and seek God for wisdom will you gain it.

Because men are successful in their worldly eyes or speak eloquently does not mean that they are wise.

"Oh, that you would be silent, and it would be your wisdom!" (Job 13:5 NKJV).

"And to man He said, 'Behold, the fear of the LORD, that is wisdom; and to depart from evil is understanding'" (Job 28:28 NASB).

"It is not only the old who are wise, not only the aged who understand what is right" (Job 32:9 NIV).

"The mouth of the righteous utters wisdom, and his tongue speaks justice. The law of his God is in his heart; his steps do not slip" (Psalm 37:30–31 ESV).

"For wisdom will come into your heart, and knowledge will be pleasant to your soul; discretion will watch over you, understanding will guard you" (Proverbs 2:10–11 ESV).

"My son, let them not depart from your eyes—keep sound wisdom and discretion; so they will be life to your soul and grace to your neck. Then you will walk safely in your way, and your foot will not stumble. When you lie down, you will not be afraid; yes, you will lie down and your sleep will be sweet" (Proverbs 3:21–24 NKJV).

"Wisdom is supreme; therefore get wisdom. Though it cost all you have, get understanding" (Proverbs 4:7 NIV).

"My son, be attentive to my wisdom; incline your ear to my understanding, that you may keep discretion, and your lips may guard knowledge" (Proverbs 5:1–2 ESV).

"For wisdom is far more valuable than rubies. Nothing you desire can compare with it" (Proverbs 8:11 NLT).

"I, wisdom, dwell together with prudence; I possess knowledge and discretion. To fear the LORD is to hate evil; I hate pride and arrogance, evil behavior and perverse speech. Counsel and sound judgment are mine; I have understanding and power" (Proverbs 8:12–14 NIV).

"Those who are wise will shine like the brightness of the heavens, and those who lead many to righteousness, like the stars for ever and ever" (Daniel 12:3 NIV).

"Oh, how I love Your law! It is my meditation all the day. You, through Your commandments, make me wiser" (Psalm 119:97–98 NKJV).

"From childhood you have known the Holy Scriptures, which are able to make you wise for salvation through faith which is in Christ Jesus" (2 Timothy 3:15 NKJV).

"The mouth of the righteous brings forth wisdom" (Proverbs 10:31 ESV).

"He who is devoid of wisdom despises his neighbor, but a man of understanding holds his peace" (Proverbs 11:12 NKJV).

"Pride only breeds quarrels, but wisdom is found in those who take advice" (Proverbs 13:10 NIV).

"The teaching of the wise is a fountain of life, that one may turn away from the snares of death" (Proverbs 13:14 ESV).

"A scoffer seeks wisdom and finds none, but knowledge is easy to one who has understanding" (Proverbs 14:6 NASB).

"How much better it is to get wisdom than gold! And to get understanding is to be chosen above silver" (Proverbs 16:16 NASB).

"The heart of the wise teaches his mouth, and adds learning to his lips" (Proverbs 16:23 NKJV).

"He who has knowledge spares his words, and a man of understanding is of a calm spirit" (Proverbs 17:27 NKJV).

"The heart of the discerning acquires knowledge; the ears of the wise seek it out" (Proverbs 18:15 NIV).

"He who gains Wisdom loves his own life; he who keeps understanding shall prosper and find good" (Proverbs 19:8 AMP).

"A man's discretion makes him slow to anger, and it is his glory to overlook a transgression" (Proverbs 19:11 NASB).

"Listen to advice and accept instruction, that you may gain wisdom in the future" (Proverbs 19:20 ESV).

"Wise words are more valuable than much gold and many rubies" (Proverbs 20:15 NLT).

"There is no wisdom, no insight, no plan that can succeed against the LORD" (Proverbs 21:30 NIV).

"Teach us to realize the brevity of life, so that we may grow in wisdom" (Psalm 90:12 NLT).

"Do not wear yourself out to get rich; have the wisdom to show restraint" (Proverbs 23:4 NIV).

"The advantage of knowledge is that wisdom preserves the life of him who has it" (Ecclesiastes 7:12 ESV).

"Wisdom brings success" (Ecclesiastes 10:10 NKJV).

"The God of our Lord Jesus Christ, the Father of glory. . . . give to you the spirit of wisdom and revelation in the knowledge of Him" (Ephesians 1:17 NKJV).

"So then do not be foolish, but understand what the will of the Lord is" (Ephesians 5:17 NASB).

"He who walks in wisdom is kept safe" (Proverbs 28:26 NIV).

"Now to the King eternal, immortal, invisible, to God who alone is wise, be honor and glory forever and ever. Amen" (1 Timothy 1:17 NKJV).

"But the wisdom from above is first pure, then peaceable, gentle, open to reason, full of mercy and good fruits, impartial and sincere" (James 3:17 ESV).

"Scorners set a city aflame, but wise men turn away anger" (Proverbs 29:8 NASB).

Chapter 68

WISE MAN VS. FOOL

Wise men talk because they have something to say; fools talk
because they have to say something.
—Plato

The fool thinks himself to be wise, but the wise man knows
himself to be a fool.
—William Shakespeare

On what are we focusing? Do we want to please man or God? Of
course we say God. But do our actions show this? Now is the
time to examine ourselves. What is the motive behind tithing, giving a
donation to a charitable organization, or helping someone? Is it about
us and how we feel or about how others feel about "generous" us? Or is
it that we should or must do this?

We must examine our motives so that we do not deceive ourselves
but are wise in our decisions.

"The wise of heart will receive commandments, but a babbling fool will come to ruin" (Proverbs 10:8 ESV).

"Whoever walks with the wise becomes wise, but the companion of fools will suffer harm" (Proverbs 13:20 ESV).

"A wise man fears the LORD and shuns evil, but a fool is hotheaded and reckless" (Proverbs 14:16 NIV).

"The crown of the wise is their riches, but the folly of fools is foolishness" (Proverbs 14:24 NASB).

"Whoever is slow to anger has great understanding, but he who has a hasty temper exalts folly" (Proverbs 14:29 ESV).

"The lips of the wise disperse knowledge, but the heart of the fool does not do so" (Proverbs 15:7 NKJV)

"The heart of him who has understanding seeks knowledge, but the mouth of fools feeds on foolishness" (Proverbs 15:14 NKJV).

"A wise son makes a father glad, but a foolish man despises his mother" (Proverbs 15:20 NKJV).

"It is better to listen to the rebuke of a wise man than for one to listen to the song of fools" (Ecclesiastes 7:5 NASB).

"The ear that listens to life-giving reproof will dwell among the wise. Whoever ignores instruction despises himself, but he who listens to reproof gains intelligence" (Proverbs 15:31–32 ESV).

"Understanding is a fountain of life to one who has it, but the discipline of fools is folly" (Proverbs 16:22 NASB).

"Wisdom is in the presence of the one who has understanding, but the eyes of a fool are on the ends of the earth" (Proverbs 17:24 NASB).

Chapter 69

WOE

W hat a powerful word—*woe*! It isn't about just feeling bad; it is about feeling overwhelmingly bad! It is a word that expresses a deep sorrow or grief. The expression "Woe is me" comes from *Hamlet* by William Shakespeare, in which Ophelia says, "Blasted with ecstasy: O, woe is me."

This word *woe* is used in the Bible, too, and will give the reader pause as to what God says will bring us woe. Our godless actions will have us saying, "O, woe is me."

"Two are better than one, because they have a good reward for their labor. For if they fall, one will lift up his companion. But woe to him who is alone when he falls, for he has no one to help him up" (Ecclesiastes 4:9–10 NKJV).

"Woe to the wicked! Disaster is upon them! They will be paid back for what their hands have done" (Isaiah 3:11 NIV).

"Woe to those who rise early in the morning, that they may run after strong drink, who tarry late into the evening as wine inflames them!" (Isaiah 5:11 ESV).

"Woe to those who draw iniquity with cords of falsehood" (Isaiah 5:18 ESV).

"Woe to those who call evil good, and good evil" (Isaiah 5:20 NKJV).

"Woe to those who are wise in their own eyes and clever in their own sight!" (Isaiah 5:21 NASB).

"Woe to men mighty at drinking wine, woe to men valiant for mixing intoxicating drink, who justify the wicked for a bribe, and take away justice from the righteous man!" (Isaiah 5:22–23 NKJV).

"Woe to the proud crown of the drunkards of Ephraim, and to the fading flower of its glorious beauty, which is at the head of the fertile valley of those who are overcome with wine!" (Isaiah 28:1 NASB).

"'Woe to the rebellious children,' says the LORD, 'who take counsel, but not of Me, and who devise plans, but not of My Spirit, that they may add sin to sin'" (Isaiah 30:1 NKJV).

"Woe to those who go down to Egypt for help, who rely on horses, who trust in the multitude of their chariots and in the great strength of their horsemen, but do not look to the Holy One of Israel, or seek help from the LORD" (Isaiah 31:1 NIV).

"Who has woe? Who has sorrow? Who has contentions? Who has complaints? Who has wounds without cause? Who has redness of eyes? Those who linger long at the wine, those who go in search of mixed wine" (Proverbs 23:29–30 NKJV).

"Woe to him who strives with his Maker!" (Isaiah 45:9 AMP).

"Woe to you . . . hypocrites! For you are like whitewashed tombs, which outwardly appear beautiful, but within are full of dead people's bones and all uncleanness" (Matthew 23:27 ESV).

Chapter 70

WORDS, SPEECH, AND COMMUNICATION

Conversation was never begun at once, nor in a hurried manner. No one was quick with a question, no matter how important, and no one was pressed for an answer. A pause giving time for thought was the truly courteous way of beginning and conducting a conversation. Silence was meaningful with the Lakota, and his granting a space of silence to the speech-maker and his own moment of silence before talking was done in the practice of true politeness and regard for the rule that "thought comes before speech."

—Luther Standing Bear, Oglala Sioux chief

Our words reveal our hearts—what we think and feel within. Before we speak, we need to think about what we are going to say. Once the words leave our mouths, we can't take them back. They are out there.

Words are powerful. They can have a positive or negative impact on a person. I can remember how the words of my English teacher had a negative impact on me when she praised my brother in front of my class. I interpreted her statement to mean that I wasn't as good as my brother. Can you imagine how a child could be devastated about being told that his parents are disappointed in him? Perhaps the parents are thinking the child performed a disappointing act, while the child thinks he is a disappointment to his parents.

When we converse with anyone, we need to choose our words wisely.

"Keep your tongue from evil and your lips from speaking lies" (Psalm 34:13 NIV).

"My tongue shall speak of Your word, for all Your commandments are righteousness" (Psalm 119:172 NKJV).

"Set a guard, O LORD, over my mouth; keep watch over the door of my lips!" (Psalm 141:3 ESV).

"Put away from you a deceitful mouth and put devious speech far from you" (Proverbs 4:24 NASB).

"The one who conceals hatred has lying lips, and whoever utters slander is a fool" (Proverbs 10:18 ESV).

"In the multitude of words sin is not lacking, but he who restrains his lips is wise. The tongue of the righteous is choice silver; the heart of the wicked is worth little. The lips of the righteous feed many, but fools die for lack of wisdom" (Proverbs 10:19–21 NKJV).

"Truthful lips endure forever, but a lying tongue lasts only a moment" (Proverbs 12:19 NIV).

"In all labor there is profit, but idle talk leads only to poverty" (Proverbs 14:23 AMP).

"A gentle answer turns away wrath, but a harsh word stirs up anger. The tongue of the wise makes knowledge acceptable, but the mouth of fools spouts folly" (Proverbs 15:1–2 NASB).

"Even a fool is counted wise when he holds his peace; when he shuts his lips, he is considered perceptive" (Proverbs 17:28 NKJV).

"A fool's mouth is his ruin, and his lips are a snare to his soul" (Proverbs 18:7 ESV).

"A false witness shall not be unpunished, and he who breathes out lies shall not escape" (Proverbs 19:5 AMP).

"He who goes about as a slanderer reveals secrets, therefore do not associate with a gossip" (Proverbs 20:19 NASB).

"He who guards his mouth and his tongue keeps himself from troubles" (Proverbs 21:23 AMP).

"Do not speak to a fool, for he will scorn the wisdom of your words" (Proverbs 23:9 NIV).

"Don't make rash promises, and don't be hasty in bringing matters before God. After all, God is in heaven, and you are here on earth. So let your words be few. Too much activity gives you restless dreams; too many words make you a fool" (Ecclesiastes 5:2–3 NLT).

"The fool multiplies words. No one knows what is coming—who can tell him what will happen after him?" (Ecclesiastes 10:14 NIV).

"With patience a ruler may be persuaded, and a soft tongue will break a bone" (Proverbs 25:15 ESV).

"A lying tongue hates its victims, and a flattering mouth works ruin" (Proverbs 26:28 ESV).

"He who rebukes a man will in the end gain more favor than he who has a flattering tongue" (Proverbs 28:23 NIV).

"Do you see a man hasty in his words? There is more hope for a fool than for him" (Proverbs 29:20 NKJV).

"But I say to you that for every idle word men may speak, they will give account of it in the day of judgment. For by your words you will be justified, and by your words you will be condemned" (Matthew 12:36–37 NKJV).

"No good tree bears bad fruit, nor does a bad tree bear good fruit. Each tree is recognized by its own fruit. People do not pick figs from thornbushes, or grapes from briers. The good man brings good things out of the good stored up in his heart, and the evil man brings evil things out of the evil stored up in his heart. For out of the overflow of his heart his mouth speaks" (Luke 6:43–45 NIV).

"Let your speech always be with grace, seasoned with salt, that you may know how you ought to answer each one" (Colossians 4:6 NKJV).

"My dear brothers, take note of this: Everyone should be quick to listen, slow to speak and slow to become angry, for man's anger does not bring about the righteous life that God desires" (James 1:19–20 NIV).

"If anyone among you thinks he is religious, and does not bridle his tongue but deceives his own heart, this one's religion is useless" (James 1:26 NKJV).

"But no one can tame the tongue; it is a restless evil and full of deadly poison. With it we bless our Lord and Father, and with it we curse men, who have been made in the likeness of God" (James 3:8–9 NASB).

Chapter 71

WORLDLINESS

I'm sure you have heard the phrase "keeping up with the Joneses." Do we buy things because we really need them or because we want to impress others? Are we in love with the world, worldly possessions, and worldly pursuits?

If we stop and turn our attention to matters of God, we will find an overwhelming contentment that cannot be derived from the world. Only God can fill us up with what is important in life.

"You shall not do at all what we are doing here today, every man doing whatever is right in his own eyes" (Deuteronomy 12:8 NASB).

"Thus says the LORD: 'Cursed is the man who trusts in man and makes flesh his strength, whose heart departs from the LORD'" (Jeremiah 17:5 NKJV).

"Their silver and gold are not able to deliver them in the day of the wrath of the LORD" (Ezekiel 7:19 ESV).

"Your heart was proud because of your beauty; you corrupted your wisdom for the sake of your splendor" (Ezekiel 28:17 ESV).

"Reproofs of discipline are the way of life, to preserve you from the evil woman, from the smooth tongue of the adulteress. Do not desire her beauty in your heart, and do not let her capture you with her eyelashes" (Proverbs 6:23–25 ESV).

"He who follows worthless pursuits is lacking in sense and is without understanding" (Proverbs 12:11 AMP).

"Neither their silver nor their gold will be able to save them on the day of the LORD's wrath" (Zephaniah 1:18 NIV).

"But He turned and said to Peter, 'Get behind Me, Satan! You are an offense to Me, for you are not mindful of the things of God, but the things of men'" (Matthew 16:23 NKJV).

"For whoever desires to save his life will lose it, but whoever loses his life for My sake will find it. For what profit is it to a man if he gains the whole world, and loses his own soul? Or what will a man give in exchange for his soul? For the Son of Man will come in the glory of His Father with His angels, and then He will reward each according to his works" (Matthew 16:25–27 NKJV).

"For whoever wishes to save his life will lose it, but whoever loses his life for My sake and the gospel's will save it. For what does it profit a man to gain the whole world, and forfeit his soul?" (Mark 8:35–36 NASB).

"A stingy man hastens after wealth and does not know that poverty will come upon him" (Proverbs 28:22 ESV).

"Then he said to them, 'Watch out! Be on your guard against all kinds of greed; a man's life does not consist in the abundance of his possessions'" (Luke 12:15 NIV).

"Rather, clothe yourselves with the Lord Jesus Christ, and do not think about how to gratify the desires of the sinful nature" (Romans 13:14 NIV).

"The idols of the nations are merely things of silver and gold, shaped by human hands" (Psalm 135:15 NLT).

"Rejoice in Christ Jesus, and have no confidence in the flesh" (Philippians 3:3 NKJV).

"Those things were important to me, but now I think they are worth nothing because of Christ" (Philippians 3:7 NCV).

"For, as I have often told you before and now say again even with tears, many live as enemies of the cross of Christ. Their destiny is destruction, their god is their stomach, and their glory is in their shame. Their mind is on earthly things" (Philippians 3:18–19 NIV).

"See to it that no one takes you captive through hollow and deceptive philosophy, which depends on human tradition and the basic principles of this world rather than on Christ" (Colossians 2:8 NIV).

"Set your mind on things above, not on things on the earth" (Colossians 3:2 NKJV).

"So put to death the sinful, earthly things lurking within you. Have nothing to do with sexual immorality, impurity, lust, and evil desires. Don't be greedy, for a greedy person is an idolater, worshiping the things of this world. Because of these sins, the anger of God is coming" (Colossians 3:5–6 NLT).

"You adulteresses, do you not know that friendship with the world is hostility toward God? Therefore whoever wishes to be a friend of the world makes himself an enemy of God" (James 4:4 NASB).

"Live for the rest of the time in the flesh no longer for human passions but for the will of God" (1 Peter 4:2 ESV).

"Do not love the world or the things in the world. If anyone loves the world, the love of the Father is not in him. For all that is in the world—the lust of the flesh, the lust of the eyes, and the pride of life—is not of the Father but is of the world. And the world is passing away, and the lust of it; but he who does the will of God abides forever" (1 John 2:15–17 NKJV).

"By this we know love, because He laid down His life for us. And we also ought to lay down our lives for the brethren. But whoever has this world's goods and sees his brother in need, and shuts up his heart from him, how does the love of God abide in him?" (1 John 3:16–17 NKJV).

"You say, 'I am rich. I have everything I want. I don't need a thing!' And you don't realize that you are wretched and miserable and poor and blind and naked" (Revelation 3:17 NLT).

Chapter 72

WORRY

Do you worry? Worry is not trusting God. We doubt the omnipotent God! In Matthew 6:25–34 and Luke 12:22–34, God gives an analogy of how He takes care of the birds, which are less in His eyes than you. It is the power of God that will take care of you, and He has promised to "supply all your need" (Philippians 4:19 NKJV).

Worry is unproductive because it obstructs clear thinking and can have adverse effects on your health. Hand your worry over to God. Surrender yourself to God. Let it go and allow God to take care of the problem. I have never heard anyone say that worrying helped the situation, and it certainly doesn't make us a martyr in the eyes of others.

I saw a greeting card that said on the outside, "Good morning, this is God" and inside, "I will be handling all your problems today. I will not need your help. So have a good day."

Don't worry, and have a good day!

"For this reason I say to you, do not be worried about your life, as to what you will eat or what you will drink; nor for your body, as to what you will put on. Is not life more than food, and the body more than clothing?" (Matthew 6:25 NASB).

"Who of you by worrying can add a single hour to his life?" (Matthew 6:27 NIV).

"So do not worry, saying, 'What shall we eat?' or 'What shall we drink?' or 'What shall we wear?'" (Matthew 6:31 NIV).

"So do not worry about tomorrow; for tomorrow will care for itself. Each day has enough trouble of its own" (Matthew 6:34 NASB).

"Then He said to His disciples, 'Therefore I say to you, do not worry about your life'" (Luke 12:22 NKJV).

"Let not your heart be troubled" (John 14:1 NKJV).

FINAL THOUGHTS

It is time that your journey begins. We know that not all journeys run smoothly. There will be bumps along the way that will help you in trusting and knowing God more intimately. Even the smooth parts of your journey will cause you to pause and joyously praise God for all of His blessings. You will know that He is with you and will never take His eyes off you. Don't take your eyes off Him.

You will find that you can pick this book up any time and read what you want to read. At different times in life, we need to read specific Scriptures that will be appropriate to us. Don't be surprised if God directs you as to what to read, and don't be afraid to ask God what you should be reading at any given time.

I would like to recommend some stories from the Bible that have had a profound impact on my life. They are all about trusting God no matter what the circumstances appear to be.

Three of the stories are in the book of Genesis. They are about Noah and the ark; Abraham, who trusted God as he was about to sacrifice his son, Isaac; and Sarah, Abraham's wife, who was promised a child by God.

Another story I love is the book of Job, which reveals a man who never gave up trusting God. I am not sure how many people today could go through what Job endured. He trusted God and not man, and he was rewarded handsomely.

In the book of Daniel is a story of three men—Shadrach, Meshach, and Abednego—who were tested for their faith in God. I had read this story many times, but one day as I was reading it I finally knew through the actions of these three men what unshakable faith is. Knowing what you can accomplish through faith is mind-boggling. When your faith starts to be questioned, read this story and meditate on it.

The Bible contains so many wonderful stories. As you read it, you will find the ones that have a significant influence on you.

If you have never read the Bible, where do you start? I would suggest that you begin by reading the book of John, Galatians, Ephesians, or Proverbs. This will help you get started learning how God thinks. Once you begin, you will want to read more books of the Bible.

I have read the Bible several times, and this is what I have discovered: a Bible passage that I had read before will all of a sudden have new meaning for me. It always astonishes me that I didn't see it before, but God knew I wasn't ready. That is one reason why you will never get tired of reading the Bible.

Another reason to read the Bible is that you will find yourself beginning to know God better. You will begin to have an intimate relationship with Him. He is your heavenly Father, and He loves you very much. Don't miss out on knowing Him. He only wants *the best for you*!

STUDY GUIDE QUESTIONS FOR DISCUSSION

1. As you read the Bible passages, which one caught your attention? You may list more than one.

   _____

   _____

   _____

   _____

   a. Why did this Bible passage catch your attention?

      _____

      _____

      _____

      _____

   b. How did (or will) this Bible passage change you?

      _____

      _____

_____

_____

2. What did you learn or relearn about God?

_____

_____

_____

3. What did you discover about Jesus?

_____

_____

_____

4. Who is the Holy Spirit, and how is He part of your life?

_____

_____

_____

5. Why is the Holy Spirit important?

_____

_____

_____

6. What did God say that surprised you? (Reference the Bible passage.)

_____

_____

_____

_____

   a. Why?

      _____

      _____

      _____

      _____

   b. Are you able to accept what He said? (Circle one.)   Yes No

   c. If not, how will you resolve this problem?

      _____

      _____

      _____

      _____

7. How will God's Word benefit you?

_____

_____

_____

_____

8. What is your favorite Bible passage?

_____

_____

_____

_____

a. Why?

_____

_____

_____

_____

b. How does this Bible passage affect you and your life?

_____

_____

_____

_____

9. Imagine that someone asked you, "What is the most important thing you received from reading God's Word?" How would you respond?

_____

_____

_____

10. Why is it important to obey God?

_____

_____

_____

_____

a. In what areas do you fail to obey God? (For example, working on the Sabbath, gossiping, or worrying)

_____

_____

_____

_____

b. Set a date when you plan to obey God in the above areas and experience His blessings.

_____

_____

_____

_____

11. Did you find a Bible passage that was difficult to believe? (Circle one.)   Yes   No

a. If yes, which one and why?

_____

_____

_____

_____

b. Remember, the entire Bible is inspired by God. Therefore, what steps will you take to believe this Bible passage?

_____

_____

_____

_____

12. What are God's specific instructions in the following areas? (Be sure to reference the Bible passage or passages pertaining to each. Feel free to add your own thoughts to the list.)

a. Tithing

_____

_____

b. Lying

_____

_____

c. Receiving blessings

_____

_____

d. Gaining wisdom

_____

_____

e. Handling disappointments

_____

_____

f. Dealing with death

_____

_____

g. Acquiring peace

_____

_____

h. Having godly friends

_____

_____

i. Forgiving

_____

_____

j. (Your thought)

_____

_____

k. (Your thought)

_____

_____

13. What will you do now to be a better you? Be specific. (Your answers from Question 12 may help you get started.)

_____

_____

_____

_____

14. When will you begin to the read the Bible?

_____

_____

15. Are you ready to change? (Circle one.)   Yes   No

a. If no, what is holding you back?

_____

_____

_____

_____

b. If yes, what steps will you take?

_____

_____

_____

_____

Appendix 2

ENDNOTES

1. Bob Holmes, "16% of US Science Teachers are Creationists." Posted May 20, 2008. www.newscientist.com (accessed November 3, 2009).
2. Hans Christian Andersen, "The Emperor's New Clothes." Posted January 28, 2010. zh.wikisource.org/wiki/en:The_Emperor's_New_Clothes (accessed March 16. 2010).
3. "Jesus is God." Modified October 21, 2009. www.allaboutjesuschrist. org. (accessed November 5, 2009).
4. Principal author: Fred de Miranda, MD, FCP, "When Human Life Begins." March 17, 2004. www.americancollegeofpediatricians. org. (accessed January 25, 2010).
5. "A Reformed Thief," an unabridged sermon by Dr. D. James Kennedy (Fort Lauderdale: Coral Ridge Ministries), 2003.

WinePressPublishing
Great Books, Defined.

To order additional copies of this book call:
1-877-421-READ (7323)
or please visit our website at
www.WinePressbooks.com

If you enjoyed this quality custom-published book,
drop by our website for more books and information.

www.winepresspublishing.com
"Your partner in custom publishing."